HOT PEPPERS

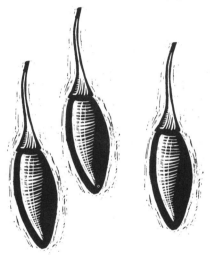

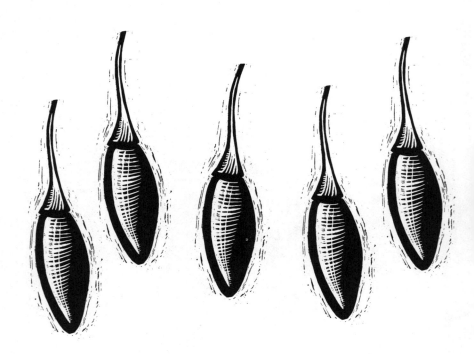

RICHARD SCHWEID

HOT PEPPERS

The Story of Cajuns and *Capsicum*

REVISED EDITION

The University of North Carolina Press Chapel Hill & London

Originally published in 1980 by Madrona Publishers.

Revised edition published in 1999 by the University of

North Carolina Press.

Designed by Richard Hendel

Set in Quadraat and Masterpiece types by Tseng Information Systems

Manufactured in the United States of America

The paper in this book meets the guidelines for permanence and
durability of the Committee on Production Guidelines for Book Longevity
of the Council on Library Resources.

Library of Congress Cataloging-in-Publication Data

Schweid, Richard, 1946–

Hot peppers : the story of Cajuns and Capsicum /

by Richard Schweid. — Rev. ed.

p.   cm.

"Chapel Hill book."

Includes bibliographical references.

ISBN 0-8078-4826-3 (pbk. : alk. paper)

1. Hot peppers.   2. Hot pepper sauce industry—Louisiana.

3. New Iberia (La.)   4. Cajuns.   I. Title.

SB307.P4S38   1999

641.3'384—dc21   99-28114

CIP

03   02   01   00   99   5   4   3   2   1

For Martha Gies and Jim Jordan

CONTENTS

ACKNOWLEDGMENTS

Thanks are due to many people who helped me with this book in many ways, at many times. Any mistakes, inaccuracies, or ill-considered conclusions herein are the responsibility of the author, but much of the energy and support needed to get the job done were provided by others. Among them were: Emmaline Broussard, Michael Burgess, Lynda Butaud, Joe Cahn, Clifford Charpentier, Charles Conte, Willie Doré, Julie Duzak, Warren Duzak, James Edmunds, Susan Hester Edmunds, John Egerton, Carole Farber, James Freedman and the Anthropology Department at the University of Western Ontario, Gene Jefferies, Robert Hester, Michelle Hoffmann, Lisa Howorth, Margaret Kleinpeter and the staff of the New Iberia Public Library, Stella Larson, Dan Levant, Raleigh Marcell, Edmund McIlhenny, Walter S. McIlhenny, Wilda Moran, the New Orleans School of Cooking, Patricia Rickles, Adele Schweid, Bernard Schweid, Ned Simmons, and Greg Tate. Special thanks to Dan Stein for the idea, to Ornella Zoia and Emanuele Nastasi for their kind support, and to Carmen Martínez for all the rest.

HOT PEPPERS

Tomorrow I'll tell you all about my stay
in New Iberia. It's a book in itself.
Henry Miller
in a letter to Anaïs Nin, January 1941

I : TO NEW IBERIA

 seeming paradox of the human condition is that pleasure and pain are parts of the same sensory spectrum, and that there is no clear division between them. Physical passion, a plunge into icy water, the heat of a steam bath, and the bite of a hot pepper are examples of things that can be experienced as either pain or pleasure, depending on the circumstances and tastes of a given individual. All of them produce sudden, sharp sensations that stimulate briefly and can be relied on to pass rapidly.

Hot peppers are used the world over to enhance almost every imaginable diet, from rice and a handful of vegetables to elaborate dishes. Their use is limited by neither race nor social class. Among the people who take pleasure from their piquancy are commoners and kings, capitalists and communists, gourmets and hobos. Archaeological evidence proves that peppers were eaten in Mexico nine thousand years ago, and they are the American continent's most popular contribution to the world's kitchen.

Despite the fact that hot peppers are indigenous to the Americas, and that certain varieties will grow well as far north as the Canadian border, there are sizable regions of the United States where their use is practically unknown. The house of my Tennessee childhood, for instance, was a meat-and-potatoes kingdom. Meals were generally seasoned with salt, pepper, and tomato catsup.

I was nineteen before I tasted hotter food. It was during a summer

trip to Mexico, in search of more exciting adventures than I was finding at college. On my first morning across the border, I was sitting at a
cafe in Nuevo Laredo with an order of eggs in front of me, wondering
how to ask for catsup in Spanish. There was a bowl on the table that
contained some sort of red sauce with seeds in it. I put a catsup-sized
portion on top of my eggs. It took five minutes for the tears to stop
streaming from my eyes, and another five to convince me that I had
done no permanent damage to the inside of my mouth. Years passed
before I tried hot sauce on my eggs again.

A decade later, many of my friends had begun to spend a good deal
of time talking about what they ate. Macrobiotic diets, health foods,
and vitamins had become common topics of conversation. These same
friends deplored my addiction to catsup. No sooner would I reach for
a bottle than someone would begin haranguing me with awful tales of
insect wings and sugar content in my daily dose.

I started looking for something to take catsup's place on my table,
and I brought home a bottle of Tabasco Sauce. It was a small bottle,
but it took me just short of six months to go through it. I began with
caution: a few drops on my eggs, or in a bowl of chili, or on French
fries. I found myself growing accustomed to the taste and gradually
my usage increased. I began putting it on stews, sauces, soups, beans,
peas, and seafood. My second bottle lasted three months. After a year,
I was using a bottle every three weeks. My catsup craving was gone and
I had acquired a hot pepper habit. I did not know it then, but about
three-quarters of the world's population shared it with me, including
millions of Americans.

I was living in Portland, Oregon, at the time, and I soon learned
that even in the cold, wet Northwest, far from tropical skies, hot sauce
could be obtained almost everywhere food was sold. I found it in convenience stores, supermarkets, hamburger heavens, barbeque joints,
chop suey houses, and the finest continental restaurants. It seemed to
be as indispensable to a bar as liquor or glasses.

I discovered that one of my neighborhood grocers was exceptionally fond of hot food. His shelves held a veritable peck of pepper
products: red and green hot sauces, mild hot sauces and hot ones, hot
sauces with preservatives and without, hot catsup, hot taco sauces,

whole peppers, diced peppers, roasted and peeled peppers, and pickled peppers.

I brought the hot sauces home, one after another, and after reading their labels, put them to the taste test. I found that each brand varied in flavor and heat. Some of the labels listed half a dozen or more ingredients, often including such items as tomatoes, dehydrated onions, and sodium benzoate, but each of the brands I came to prefer contained only red peppers, vinegar, and salt. My three favorites were Tabasco Sauce, Mexi-Pep, and Louisiana Hot Sauce. Each was manufactured by a different company, but according to the labels all three companies were located in the same place: New Iberia, Louisiana.

New Iberia is in southern Louisiana, about halfway between Mississippi and Texas, close to the Gulf of Mexico. I had scanty but colorful ideas about the region: Cajuns, bayous, swamps, gumbo, zydeco music, and the French language. I imagined the area held an ethnic group of fifth- and sixth-generation Americans who were still resisting assimilation into the national culture, a self-sufficient people, maintaining a distinct and peculiar way of life, far removed from the mainstream. I had, in short, suspected the existence of a foreign country there, within the borders of the United States. I was not surprised that the best hot sauces I could find were all made in New Iberia.

I had driven through New Orleans on a number of cross-country journeys, but had never taken the time to explore southern Louisiana. I knew it would not be enough simply to cruise through and see the sights. I wanted to stay long enough to get a feeling for how life was being lived. It is not considered good form to lounge around small southern towns and conspicuously do nothing for a couple of months, unless one is old enough to be retired. Why not take up the trail of the hot pepper and see where it led? I equipped my Toyota for the trip with four new tires and a tune-up, and set out for New Orleans in the autumn of 1978.

At that time, the road from New Orleans to New Iberia, state highway 90W, passed through two urban centers: Houma and Morgan City. The forty-mile ride between them lived up to my expectations of bayou country. A highway in name only, the chuck-holed two lanes snaked along a narrow corridor. A wall of sugar cane, ten feet high, was on the left and Bayou Black flowed slowly on the right.

At the water's edge were ramshackle wooden cabins, mounted on cement blocks by way of foundations. Beside almost every house rested a small, overturned flat-bottomed wooden boat. Occasionally, one of them lay abandoned, pulled up halfway on the bank, its stern filling with water as the bayou slowly claimed it. Huge live oaks grew along the banks. Their thick, gnarled branches, beribboned with Spanish moss, stretched out over the muddy water.

This feeling of backwater isolation ended abruptly at Morgan City, forty-five miles east of New Iberia. Here, in the seat of Saint Mary's Parish (in Louisiana, counties are called parishes), a different aspect of life in southern Louisiana presented itself. Morgan City is connected by the Atchafalaya (pronounced a-chaff-a-lie-a) River to the Gulf of Mexico, and at that time it was a thriving center of the petroleum industry. Highway 90 had been expanded to four lanes and was lined with industrial satellites: shipyards, dry docks, tool companies, equipment companies, big trucks, and construction machinery. Traffic was heavy and dust hung thick in the air.

The rest of the nation was in an economic slump, with increasing inflation and rapidly rising interest rates, but southern Louisiana was in the middle of an unprecedented boom. Oil was selling at upwards of $40 a barrel, and the prosperity generated by the petroleum industry was touching the lives of almost everyone in the state. When the oil patch was booming, there was work for anyone willing and able to do it, and many people were packing up and heading to Louisiana in search of jobs.

Commercials on the radio in Baltimore, Pittsburgh, Youngstown, and Detroit were announcing that such-and-such a company in Morgan City, Louisiana needed shipfitters, welders, pipefitters, or electricians. The commercials described the subtropical climate, touted the area's hunting and fishing, and enumerated the eight to thirteen dollars an hour plus company benefits that went along with the jobs. Such advertisements touched the quick of young workers in northern industrial cities who were trying to cope with periodic unemployment, bitter winters, and rising prices.

World demand for oil had transformed the economy and the people in Morgan City and New Iberia as dramatically as in Saudi Arabia or Kuwait. As the oil had been pumped out, the twentieth century had come pouring in, with all its pleasures, pollutants, and paranoias. Large numbers of unemployed strangers suddenly descended on the area. Nobody knew where they came from, or what they had done there, or why they had wanted to leave. Some, at least, were from neighboring southern states, but large numbers came from outside of Dixie. Southern Louisiana had always had its share of transient workers, but they were agricultural laborers and their residency was seasonal. The oil industry, however, always needed a pair of hands to push, pull, wind, shove, and haul. Men who filled these positions were called roustabouts, and there were never enough of them. The pay was good and there was always plenty of overtime.

On any stretch of Highway 90, in those days, there were usually a few solitary hitchhikers, roustabouts who either were on their way to board a ship and head out to an oil platform or had just come back on land and were thumbing their way to wherever they called home. On the western edge of Morgan City, I picked up a stocky, middle-aged man of medium height, dressed in work boots, a clean white shirt, and pressed slacks. He was carrying a small flight bag. He noticed my Oregon license plates and asked, in a slow southern drawl, where I was going.

I explained that I had come to do research on hot peppers. He gave me a sidelong glance, as if to find out whether his leg was being pulled. "Hot peppers? Well, ah'll be damned. Seems like a right far piece to travel jist to find out about 'em. They shore use a lot of 'em around here. Man, they do love that hot food."

He was from Mississippi. "We eat a right smart amount of hot food over there, but nothin' like these Cajuns. You can drop me in Jeanerette. Ah lef' mah car with mah brother when ah went offshore. He lives in Jeanerette. Tha's how ah come to be here. Mah brother wrote and said come on over, there's plenty of work. He was right about that.

"Ah jist got in from the Gulf. Been out fourteen days. Could have stayed out another seven, but what the hell? Ah already cleared over five hunnerd dollars for the las' two weeks. Anybody with two arms and two legs can find work here. They're beggin' for people, but in mah part of Mississippi there ain't nothin' happenin'. Hell, ah had to come over the firs' time on a bus, and now ah got me a '73 Pontiac, a damn nice car. Ah ain't cleared less'n a thousand a month since ah been here, and some months it's been more."

I dropped him at his brother's trailer home on the outskirts of Jeanerette (pronounced *gin-erette*). He pointed proudly to the big car parked there, waiting for him. "Not too good on gas, but she'll go lak a bat outta hell. 'Preciate the ride. Good luck with your hot peppers," he added dubiously.

The nineteen miles of road between Jeanerette and New Iberia ran through land that was under extensive cultivation, but there was not a hot pepper in sight. Every field was planted in sugar cane, narrow row after narrow row of ten-foot stalks, which stretched away across the flat ground toward the horizon. Sugar cane has been the economic backbone of Iberia Parish for most of this century. In 1978, more acres of cane were still being grown in the parish than all other agricultural crops combined, but sugar cane ranked second, behind the petroleum industry, as a revenue producer for the fifth year in a row.

In the midst of the region's petro prosperity sugar cane farmers were suffering. Three of the area's thirty-one sugar cane mills had closed and others were expected to follow suit. More and more farmers were planting their cane fields in soybeans or rice. Inflation was increasing the overhead for both growers and mills, and the oil patch was draining available labor. Competition in the world sugar market had become increasingly devastating. Cane farmers were insisting that it cost them sixteen cents to grow a pound of cane, but Congress had refused to set price supports above fourteen and a half cents. Despite all of that, there were over forty thousand acres of cane planted in Iberia Parish in 1977, worth about $17 million.

By 1986, less than a decade later, New Iberia's economy had gone through a 180-degree change. The petroleum boom had gone bust, but in the midst of 20 percent unemployment and southern Louisiana's worst economy since the Depression, cane farmers were doing well, thanks to the Reagan administration's price supports of eighteen cents a pound. In 1985, revenue from the cane crop in Iberia Parish was worth $39 million, and by 1997 it was worth almost $43.5 million.

I did not know anything about the economics of sugar cane as I was driving into New Iberia for the first time, but it was plain enough that hot peppers were not the sun around which the area's agricultural life revolved. As I drove by acre after acre of towering cane, I was disappointed not to see peppers growing in every field as I had expected to, but I knew that many a journey had begun with a mistaken expectation and proceeded to uncover wonders far greater than could have been imagined. It was, in fact, just such a mistaken expectation by Christopher Columbus that introduced hot peppers to the Old World.

*

When he returned to Spain from the West Indies in 1493, Columbus brought the first hot peppers ever seen in Europe. There is no mention of them in Chinese, Sanskrit, Egyptian, Greek, Arabic, or Latin. Moreover, there is no record of them in any European accounts of Asia, Arabia, or Africa before the sixteenth century. It is assumed they grew exclusively in the Americas.

The first recorded mention of hot peppers is in Columbus's journal of his first voyage. The original manuscript has been destroyed, but Bartolomeo de Las Casas's abstract, which has survived, is believed to be a close copy. The entry for Wednesday, January 2, 1493, reads: "The spicery that they eat, says the Admiral [Columbus], is abundant and more valuable than black pepper or grains of paradise [pepper from Portuguese Guinea]. He left a recommendation to those whom he wished to leave there, that they should get as much as they could."

The voyage of Admiral Columbus and his three ships cost a tremendous amount of money to prepare and provision. Spain's sovereigns, Ferdinand and Isabella, expected a substantial return on their investment. Their greatest hope was for gold. Columbus found a small amount, but it was in the form of ornaments belonging to individuals. He received reports of places where gold was abundant, but had neither time nor money to verify them. He returned to Spain with only a few pieces of jewelry and the unproved certainty that great riches awaited discovery.

Second only to the precious metal, Ferdinand and Isabella hoped for black pepper. When Marco Polo had returned from the Orient in 1295, he brought black pepper with him. By 1492, it commanded a high price on the spice-hungry markets of Europe. Black pepper belongs to the genus *Piper*. Hot and sweet peppers both belong to the genus *Capsicum*, a name that is thought to have come from the Greek verb *kapto*, meaning "I bite" (literally, "I gulp down"), or, as others consider more likely, from the Latin word *capsa*, which means capsule or pod. Black pepper is completely unrelated to hot peppers.

Since Columbus did not turn up so much as one grain of black pepper, he was eager to promote the commercial possibilities of the hot peppers that he had found growing in such profusion. He wrote enthusiastically of them in his journal entry for January 15, 1493: "The land was found to produce much *aji*, which is the pepper of the inhabitants, and more valuable than the common sort; they deem it very wholesome and eat nothing without it. Fifty caravels [large ships] might be loaded every year with this commodity."

The glowing expectations that Columbus held for the future of hot peppers were quickly justified, but it was too late for the admiral. He died in 1506, aging, bitter, and unrewarded. Shortly before his death, Columbus wrote to his son Diego: "I have received nothing of the revenue due me, but live by borrowing. Little have I profited by twenty years of toils and perils, since at present I do not own a roof in Spain. I have no resort but an inn, and, for the most times, have not wherewithal to pay my bill."

The word *aji* (pronounced *ah-hee*) was incorporated into the Spanish language and is used to this day to mean hot peppers. South Americans adopted the relatively young language of their conquerors, but *aji* was an ancient word that they planted in the Spanish tongue like a strong, enduring seed. It took root and flourished in much the same way that the hot peppers it denoted thrived in the European culture.

Within fifty years after Columbus introduced *Capsicum* to the Old

World, its use was widespread. Shops carried a variety of hot peppers. They were grown in gardens and used as both food and medicine. They had also reached Asia. As early as 1542, three varieties were reported growing in Goa, on the southwestern coast of India, where they had arrived with the Portuguese. The speed with which hot peppers spread around the globe is unequalled in the annals of food. Never have so many different cultures embraced a food so rapidly.

By the seventeenth century, hot peppers were common in the most far-flung places in the world, their universal appeal paralleled only by that of tobacco. Hot peppers and tobacco both belong to the family of plants called Solanaceae. Both were American plants brought to Europe by Columbus. The similarities of their histories will come as no surprise to those who crave hot peppers, because they are well aware of the extent to which this craving can become an addiction.

By the eighteenth century, the use of hot peppers in Asia was so common that many travelers, both Oriental and Occidental, assumed Capsicum was native to the Orient and had been in Asia prior to 1492. Contemporary botanists, however, are almost unanimous in the opinion that only three plants were used in both the Orient and the Americas before Columbus: the bottle-gourd, the coconut, and the sweet potato. This, plus the fact that Spanish and Portuguese explorers are known to have frequently carried plants and seeds from one part of the world to another, has led scholars to the conclusion that Capsicum was unknown outside of the Americas before Columbus.

A variety of reasons can be offered to explain why people took so readily to hot peppers. Among them is that they spice up a bland or limited diet. Hot peppers and salt are the two most commonly used seasonings in the world. It is also true that food was valuable and often scarce. There was no refrigeration. People could not afford to throw away leftovers that were only slightly rotten, and Capsicum helped to cover the taste of food that was past its prime.

Hot peppers are high in both vitamin A and vitamin C. There are 77,000 units of vitamin A, about fifteen times the minimum daily requirement, in one-quarter of a pound of peppers, and over 160 milligrams of vitamin C, which is four times the minimum daily requirement, in one-tenth of a pound. There were very few sources of these vitamins available to most people during the sixteenth and seventeenth centuries, and it is possible that the body's own wisdom created a craving for hot peppers.

These are some of the standard possibilities usually raised by ethnobotanists. They are all plausible, and perhaps each is true, but none is wholly satisfactory. *Capsicum* was so readily accepted because human beings everywhere recognized it as a special plant possessing unique qualities. Wild peppers were picked and eaten in Mexico before the people there were even planting seeds. The intensity of their color —almost all peppers ripen to a bright red—and the heat of their taste have always proven to be powerfully attractive. *Capsicum* is one of America's primal foods.

t was early October, but the sun blazed down. By the time I reached New Iberia, the back of my shirt was stuck to the driver's seat. My first stop was a supermarket in a shopping center on the eastern edge of town. I eagerly cased the produce section, but cayennes were the only hot peppers represented. I looked on the shelf for hot sauces and found three brands, each made in New Iberia, but all wearing the labels I had seen all over the United States. Nothing special. I bought a cold bottle of orange juice and drove into town.

I headed west on Main Street, toward downtown. Main Street used to be called the Old Spanish Trail. People have been using it to get to New Iberia for two hundred years. As its name indicates, New Iberia was founded by Spaniards. From 1765 to 1803, Spain owned the Louisiana territory and Spanish émigrés came over by the shipload. When they arrived, they followed the trail from New Orleans out into the empty reaches of southern Louisiana, stopping when they found a place they liked.

New Iberia was established by a group from Malaga in 1779. Many landholders in Iberia Parish today are descendants of the first groups of Spanish settlers. There are more Seguras and Romeros in the New Iberia phone book than Joneses or Smiths.

I drove past three white antebellum mansions, columned and corniced. They had all been built on the north side of the street, with the Old Spanish Trail in front of them and the Bayou Teche (pronounced *tesh*), which runs through New Iberia paralleling Main Street, behind them. Their back yards sloped gently down to the bayou. Each house had a vast lawn shaded by massive live oaks. These architectural marvels of the Old South were built by cotton and sugar barons who used them as townhouses in the 1830s and 1840s.

Half a block past the last manse, called the Shadows on the Teche, downtown began in earnest. There was a boarded-up movie theater, a sewing machine store, and a discount clothing store. The old brick buildings looked tired and sooty. Most of downtown New Iberia dated from around 1900, having been rebuilt after a terrible fire in 1899 burned some 120 buildings to the ground. The downtown New Iberia that I saw consisted of about ten blocks of two-story buildings along Main Street, with storefronts on the bottom floors and empty second stories with dusty, opaque windows.

I parked on Main Street and went into Provost's Bar and Grill. It was high-ceilinged, dim, and cool. A massive mahogany bar ran the length of one side of the room, a huge oak-framed mirror on the wall behind it.

The daily special was written on the chalkboard: pork chops, rice, greens, salad, bread, and coffee: $2.15. The jukebox against the far wall had the standard country and western selections, including some fine Hank Williams classics, as well as records by Fats Domino and Clifton Chenier. I dropped in a quarter and heard one of each.

The white man behind the bar was dressed in blue jeans and a white shirt. His sleeves were rolled up and he had on a long white apron, tied around his middle. He was short, muscular, and appeared to be in his mid-forties. He was clean-shaven, both his face and his head. The tan of his scalp indicated it had been that way for some time. He brought my food, and I noticed there were two bottles of hot sauce on the table. One was the regular red mixture and the other was a bottle stuffed full of short green peppers covered with vinegar. This hot vinegar was perfect for my greens. The coffee was dark and strong.

I lingered over the meal and pondered the problem of lodging. I had passed a few motels on the edge of town near the shopping center, but they had not appealed to me. I was not looking for a faceless motel room. I wanted a place that would remind me where I was, walls that exhaled the air of New Iberia, not mindless designs of concrete and right angles drafted in New York or Los Angeles and sent to a local contractor.

The bartender asked me, "Who do you think's gonna win the World Series?"

I told him that my heart was with the Dodgers but my money was on the Yankees.

He wiped down the spotless dark wood of the bar. It was two in the afternoon and we were alone amidst the empty stools, tables, and shadows. "That's how I feel about it," he said. "Of course, the Yankees got that Cajun boy pitchin' for them, Ron Guidry, from right over here in Lafayette. Still, I hate to see them win. They've got so much money it's like they bought the pennant, you know? Nobody around here is crazy about the Yankees, but they're gonna be mighty hard to beat. Just passin' through?"

I explained that I was planning to stay a while and do some research on hot peppers. I asked if he knew of a nearby boarding house.

"A boarding house? I reckon not. Hasn't been one for quite a few years. Closest thing would be the Teche Hotel on the west end of town, but they don't serve food. I guess you'll learn a lot about hot peppers around here. Folks eat 'em with everything. Trappey's hot sauce company is right up the street, and you could go over to Avery Island and talk to the McIlhennys. They make Tabasco Sauce. My name's Richard Provost," he said.

I noted the opening and closing times at Provost's and drove through town to the Teche Hotel. It was a large old two-story house that had been broken up into rooms many years before. I rented a light, spacious room with a bath and five windows for twenty-five dollars a week. The middle-aged landlady, who introduced herself as Miz Marie, assured me, "You're lucky to get it. This room just opened up today. Any other place in town would charge you three times as much for a room half as big and the bath would be in the hall. And you'd be lucky to find that, *cher*. There's more people in this town than there are rooms for them to rent, and that's the truth."

Even before the offshore oil boom, and long after it had passed, there was no shortage of guests at the Teche Hotel. There was always an old pensioner or two who needed cheap, clean lodgings close to town; and the drummers—traveling salesmen—came through year round. My room was on the second floor, at the top of the broad, carpeted stairs. The wood of the banister was smoothed by many years of hands, and the carpet was growing thin where so many weary feet had dragged on their way up to a night's sleep at the Teche.

An easy chair beside one of the windows in my room looked out over a shed with a corrugated tin roof. A rusty Coca-Cola sign was nailed to its side. At one end of the shed was a tall palm tree, at the other a bunch of broad-leafed banana plants. The vista could have been any tropical town between Louisiana and Brazil.

*

I used the pay phone in the hotel lobby to begin calling around and making appointments. I found myself, finally, talking to people who were not in the least surprised that anyone might be researching something so common and ordinary as hot peppers. The Trappeys and the McIlhennys were immediately enthusiastic and cooperative.

I went out in search of an evening meal as the sun was setting. A two-minute walk south from the hotel carried me across a set of railroad tracks and into the black section of town, which local whites call the Southside. Some of the streets were covered with shells, practically the last unpaved streets in New Iberia. Much of the ground in Iberia Parish is soft and swampy. Clamshells are more plentiful than gravel and are often used to cover sidewalks, driveways, and unpaved streets. Every time a car passed, it sent up clouds of white dust.

The houses on the Southside were small and wooden, raised on foundations of cement blocks. The yards were neat and planted in a subtropical abundance of palmettos, gardenias, fig trees, magnolias, mimosas, and pecan trees. The lawns were bordered with a ground cover of things like the purple, long-leafed wandering Jew, a favorite of houseplant enthusiasts in Oregon. In New Iberia, it grows outdoors in profuse tendrils, sporting tiny white blossoms and creeping along the edge of flower beds full of zinnias and snapdragons.

Two boys were washing a small brown mongrel dog in a tin tub on the steps of their front porch. One of the kids knelt down and held the shivering, howling dog, while the other held the hose. Both boys were

In the Teche Hotel

spindly, just coming into their growth, all arms and legs and scraps of faded tan shorts. The dog managed to jump from the tub and began shaking itself, sending a fan of dark drops across the gray, weathered, pine porch steps. The dog cowered beneath a bush in the front yard.

It was a pepper bush! It stood about three feet high and was loaded with short red peppers that stood erect, growing up from the branches. I didn't know it then, but I was looking at a variety of the species *Capsicum frutescens*, which is the hottest pepper grown in the United States. It will grow in only a handful of North American locales, and it grows best in the area around Iberia Parish. This is the kind of pepper that the McIlhenny Company uses to make Tabasco Sauce, and the people of southern Louisiana call it a tabasco pepper.

Further along was a wooden weighing shed with a large scale beside its doorway and a sign advertising that the proprietor was paying forty-five cents a pound for pecans. People lounged outside their houses on porch swings and rocking chairs in the twilight. Greetings exchanged with people walking by drifted through the evening air: "Hey there, how y'all doin'?"

The light was gone and night had fallen. I stopped for dinner at Moore's Cafe, a modest establishment by the railroad tracks, whose quality, sizable portions, coffee, and prices rivaled Provost's. I began to enjoy a great confidence that I would have no trouble feeding my face to my heart's content in New Iberia.

My waiter was an older man, perhaps Mr. Moore himself. I never asked. He had skin the color of well-polished mahogany and tight curls of gray hair. He was short, thin, and dapper. Despite the fact that the cafe was patronized almost exclusively by workers from the neighborhood who wore the green cottons or blue denims of their trades, he was dressed in the vest and slacks from a three-piece suit of soft gray wool. His white shirt was starched and gleaming, the sleeves bunched at his biceps by delicate black silk garters. A diamond stickpin was in his tie and he wore gold cufflinks. His feet were shod in formal black pumps with a high polish and dark socks so thin I could see his ankles through them.

When he had set my coffee down, he asked who I liked in the World Series. After a bit, our talk turned to hot peppers. "Plenty of 'em down here," he assured me. "I mind when this time of year you used to see 'em in every field, acres of 'em turnin' red. That's how it used ter be. Folks around here still be crazy 'bout 'em, though they don't grow many any more. Eat 'em on most anything. I'm right fond of hot food myself. I go through one of those little bottles of hot sauce every couple of weeks. I reckon it heps keep me healthy."

*

The roots of that reckoning extend deep into prehistory. From the archaeological digs at Tehuacan, 150 miles south of Mexico City, have come the remains of hot peppers preserved in human coprolites (fossilized excrement) believed to be over nine thousand years old. This predates the first known cultivation of plants in Mexico by fifteen hundred years, so it must be assumed that these were wild peppers.

There is a school of thought that believes the best way to study the evolution of the human race is to examine the development of the means by which people get sustenance from their environment. To stay in one place and cause your food to grow is a process that indicates a far more civilized social order than one based on the necessity of chasing, killing, and eating whatever living thing crosses your path — be it bird, boar, or spider. It appears likely that hot peppers, with a handful of other plants such as beans and corn, played a critical role in this transition for the people who lived around Tehuacan. Remains of cultivated *Capsicum* at the site have been dated back to 5500 B.C.

Archaeological evidence of early hot pepper cultivation in South America comes from the Huaca Prieta mound, a site along the coast of northern Peru whose habitation has been dated to around 2000 B.C. The remains of various foods and plants are often found in ancient graves, and it is common, in both Tehuacan and Huaca Prieta, to find fragments of hot peppers in burial sites. Although most scholars decline to speculate why these things accompanied the dead, it is safe to say there was a special and intense relationship between primitive peoples and the peppers they grew.

It is possible to know which plants people ate in pre-Columbian America, but it is not possible to know why they ate them, or how they perceived the plants. It is not possible to determine how much of their use was as food and how much as medicine. The available data is entirely archaeological until the arrival of the Spaniards in the middle 1500s. The Spaniards noted that the Maya of southern Mexico and northern Guatemala had at least five words for hot peppers.

The Mayan priests had written many volumes in their strange hieroglyphs, detailing their sophisticated body of knowledge, including observations on agriculture, medicine, weaponry, science, and religion. Bishop Landa (may his name be reviled all the days of the world!), the third bishop of the Yucatan following the Spanish conquest, wrote: "We found . . . a great number of these books written with their characters, and we burned them all, which they [the Mayan priests] felt most deeply, and over which they showed much sorrow."

Bishop Landa's self-righteous fire destroyed most of the written records of pre-Columbian culture on the American continent. Fortunately, during the next two centuries, a handful of Spanish clergy took considerable steps to preserve what evidence could be gathered through oral interviews about Mayan society and its attitudes toward the cosmos. Particular attention was paid to medical practices and the plants that made up the Mayan pharmacopoeia. This information was set down in Latin, sent to Rome, and deposited in the Vatican archives.

In 1931, Dr. Ralph Roys, then at Tulane University, gathered this data together in his book *Ethnobotany of the Maya*. From his work, it is clear that *Capsicum* played an important and well-defined role in the healing system of the Maya. Many of the same medicinal qualities in hot peppers that were recognized then are still being exploited today.

In the introduction to his book, Dr. Roys cautioned readers against viewing the Mayan pharmacopoeia as simply superstition: ". . . we find a surprisingly large percentage of the Maya medical texts devoted to the treatment of symptoms and based on objective observations of the effects of certain plants on the human system. Maya medicine at least was not hampered by the theories of humors and distempers which so long continued to be the basis of European medical science."

Hot pepper, taken internally, was the treatment of choice among the Maya for asthma and stubborn coughs. In 1978, Dr. Irwin Ziment, a California lung specialist, announced that he had found *Capsicum* to be of use in stimulating secretions in the respiratory tract that assisted in bringing up sputum. He recommended gargling with a few drops of Tabasco Sauce. *Capsicum* is a mucokinetic agent, i.e., it stimulates the mucous membranes and causes the nose to run, the eyes to water, and coughing, sneezing, and expectoration to commence.

The chemical in hot peppers that is responsible for their heat is called capsaicin (pronounced *cap-say-i-sin*), $C_{18}H_{27}N_3$. It is potent enough to be detected by the human tongue when as little as one part capsaicin is present in one hundred thousand parts water. The Mayan prescription for aching bones and muscles was a paste that contained the crushed pepper called *chac-ic*, an exceptionally hot pepper that was probably similar to tabasco peppers. The paste was applied and covered with leaves from a pepper bush. Contemporary pharmaceutical companies are still turning out analogues of the old Mayan nostrums with products like Heet and Sloan's Liniment, whose principal effective ingredient is oleoresin of capsaicin. Hot pepper oil.

The Maya treated a sore throat with a mash of the *chac-ic* pepper, which was used as a poultice or diluted and taken internally. Today, Parke-Davis manufactures a product called Throat Discs, which also uses oleoresin of capsaicin as its active ingredient. The heat loosens muscles in the gorge and draws attention away from the discomfort.

Problems with bad teeth and soft gums plague people who live in tropical climates. For inflamed gums, the Maya crushed the roots of three different kinds of hot peppers and boiled them with five *chac-ic* peppers. This they wrapped in cotton wool and held it, while still warm, to the afflicted gum.

In the north of Mexico, practically the same procedure for gum trouble was recommended by the Aztecs, who also cultivated *Capsicum*. References to it can be found in the *Badianus Manuscript*, an herbal written in 1552 by an Aztec physician and translated into Latin by another Aztec who was known as Badianus. The Aztecs had at least seven different words meaning hot pepper. Among them were *quauchilli*, *zenalchilli*, and *chiltecpin*. This is, obviously, the origin of the word *chili*.

By the time Christopher Columbus found the people of the West Indies eating hot peppers, they had probably been doing so for centuries. There are two ways *Capsicum* might have spread throughout the Caribbean: through traders from Mexico or South America, or by the animal kingdom's great seed dispersal agents, the birds. Many kinds of birds favor hot peppers, and in the tropics birds can be seen flying down to pluck them from the bush. The seeds pass whole through the avian digestive tract and are excreted. Often they fall into soil where they thrive.

*

I ended my first day in New Iberia back at the Teche Hotel, sitting in the lobby with Lee and Burt, two other residents of the Teche, drinking Dixie Beer and watching the first game of the World Series. Lee drove big trucks for a living, hauling all over Louisiana and Texas. Burt worked "seven and seven" (seven days on, seven days off) on a ship that serviced offshore oil rigs. Both were in their early twenties. Lee had refused my offer to pay him for the first beer by handing me a second one.

A man came in and strode directly to the pay phone at the far end of the lobby. The phone was mounted on the wall. Anyone sitting in front of the television could hear the Teche end of a phone conversation, unless the caller faced the wall and spoke softly.

This man's name was Al, and he was from Jackson, Mississippi. Tall and broad, in his early forties, he had a mean face under close-cut, steel-gray hair. He worked long hours at a nearby machine shop. Every evening he would come back to the hotel in his pickup truck, go to his room, bathe, descend the stairs wearing clean jeans and a white shirt, and drive to a franchise restaurant a few blocks away, where, he once told me, he ate a steak dinner every night.

He placed his call, through an operator, to Pascagoula, Mississippi, and his voice overrode the noise at Dodger Stadium. "Look here now, baby, how is it that if we're engaged you can let some guy come around and do those things to ya? Christ almighty, I gave you that ring, I thought we were gonna get married, and now I come to find out ya been letting that go on. He's probably there slobberin' on ya right now, ain't he?"

He went on for about ten minutes, increasingly loud and enraged. Then, suddenly, he stopped in mid-sentence. It was clear that one woman in Pascagoula, Mississippi, had just hung up her phone.

Al stood there a moment, cursing, then stalked toward the stairs. He stopped by Lee's chair. Lee was not big, but he came on tough and fearless. He looked into Al's narrowed, angry eyes and started to laugh. I had an instant's flow of adrenaline, expecting Al to go berserk. He only scowled and whined sourly, "Three hundred and fifty dollars I spent on that ring. Can you believe it? Well, if y'all are gonna watch this goddamned baseball, I guess I'll jist go on up to bed."

It was a good game. The Dodgers took it 4-1.

ot peppers are habit-forming. Everyone I spoke to who was in any way connected with them agreed. Consumers, growers, botanists, and hot sauce manufacturers all noted that when people begin to use hot peppers in their food, they soon reach a point where they cannot enjoy a meal without them. Food seems dull, bland, and monotonous. The appetite diminishes. The pleasures of the table become dependent on the stimulating rush of hot peppers.

There are an increasing number of North Americans who are experimenting with hot foods, and many of these people subsequently become avid users. Each year, hot sauce manufacturers report an expanded market for their products. Hot peppers are a valuable commodity: in 1977 the hot pepper harvest in the United States was worth about $60 million, in 1985 it was valued at around $135 million, and by 1998 the figure had climbed to well over $200 million and *salsa picante* replaced catsup as the nation's favorite condiment.

A farmer in southern Louisiana who grows a hundred acres of hot peppers can make as much money as one who grows five hundred acres of sugar cane. If, that is, people can be found to pick the peppers when they are ripe. Fewer and fewer people are willing to do this kind of work. While researchers at Texas A&M University were claiming, in 1986, to have finally developed a cost-effective mechanical harvester for peppers, after years of efforts by industry and universities in both Louisiana and the Southwest to come up with one, the machine is designed for harvesting a tough-skinned pepper called the Tam-Mild

Jalapeño #1, and it is of no use in farming either tabasco peppers or cayennes, the two types of pepper most frequently grown in Louisiana. So despite an increasing national demand and a rising market value, the number of farmers in Iberia Parish who grow hot peppers on a commercial basis has dwindled to almost none.

During the first half of this century, many of the region's small farmers grew a few acres of cayennes, or tabascos, or sport peppers, which they sold to the McIlhennys or the Trappeys. Pepper-picking season stretched from July to December, depending on which of these three varieties was being picked. The hot pepper harvest used to make a substantial impact on the economy of Iberia Parish.

Stella Larson was a lifelong resident of the area. She remembered when living revolved around hot peppers: "When I was a kid my family were sharecroppers. We'd get six cents for a gallon of peppers [four pounds to a gallon]. We used to plant many acres. Just my daddy and us children to work it. We'd start at four-thirty in the morning and get done when it got dark. Pepper—that's all we had to pay our bills. You could live almost a whole year on a hundred-dollar bill in the country, if you had hogs and chickens."

She was a thin, middle-aged woman with pale skin, dark hair, and intense brown eyes. She had a fierce energy and was constantly moving, thinking, talking, trying to figure out what was going on in the world around her. When we met, she was working as a waitress in the restaurant of a fancy motel just outside of New Iberia.

"When we picked those tabasco peppers, we would burn our hands. And I do mean burn, *cher*. Have to lay 'em in a bowl of cool milk at night. When I was a child, I'd cry all night long after pickin' 'em during the day, but I could pick more'n anybody else.

"Then my daddy took to growin' sport peppers. Sports are not as large as cayennes, and not so small as tabascos. They're an in-between size. They were called sports because they didn't burn your hand when you picked them. Also, a sport pepper looks like somebody dressed up in a nice, new suit. That's just how it looks. But a tabasco pepper is hell on earth, *cher*. I must say we were awfully glad when my daddy switched from tabasco to sport. After that came cayennes, and they didn't burn you either."

In southern Louisiana, hot peppers are started in greenhouses around mid-January. The plant is a perennial, but because it hybridizes easily from year to year, farmers like to start each year's plants from seed. By late March, the peppers are transferred to the open fields. Cayennes will begin to ripen in three months, sports in three and a half, and tabascos in four. The pepper bushes continue to produce fruit until the first frost.

A greenhouse is not cheap, and in the old days farmers like Stella Larson's father often had to improvise. "We'd punch out holes in the bottom of the same kind of round tin tub we used for baths, and start the peppers in there. That way the water would run out the bottom and you could cover the seedlings with a blanket when it got really cold. That March wind can be awful bad for the farmer. It used to blow away the seed and we'd have to start sowin' all over again. That's why my daddy took to raisin' 'em ahead of time. Then we'd get out in the mud up to our neck, *cher*, and set out those pepper plants. Lord, that was so much fun."

Since all of the pepper pods on any given bush do not come ripe at the same time, a field can be picked eight or nine times during an average season. "This was how it worked—most of the time you were just interested in the ripe peppers. Sometimes Trappey's would buy the green tabascos to put up in vinegar, but not all the time. So you'd be goin' through the fields pickin' the ripe ones. By the time you got to the end of the field, you'd have to come back and start again in that same field. That's how fast they came ripe.

"We'd go out there barefooted and cold. Those chilly mornings were something. We'd have syrup cake and boiled potato for breakfast. My daddy had a hundred gallons of cane syrup made at the mill every year for us. Syrup cake is sort of like gingerbread, but it's much more delicious. I think they make some kind of bread similar to it in India."

Her voice grew wistful. "We were fifteen children. It was good days. We didn't know there was another life. A lot of the time I wish we could go back on the farm. My memories of my childhood are really the only riches I have. The best time of my life was pickin' pepper. That, and riding in a wagon of cotton, or goin' into the woods to look for firewood."

She had watched the traditions and beliefs that were familiar to her as a child pass entirely out of existence in the span of her lifetime. She mourned the old ways of life. Her contemporaries had all watched and participated in the same process. Most of them remembered those days with fondness but believed progress had been made and the quality of life had improved. Stella Larson was unusual in that she was not so sure.

What happened in her lifetime was that southern Louisiana joined the United States. For almost two centuries, these parishes enjoyed a favorable balance of trade with the rest of the world. Products like cotton, sugar cane, seafood, furs, and hot peppers were in demand on national and international markets, but there was little that Cajuns needed to buy from the rest of the world. Almost everything they wanted was available close to home, and most of it they grew, or trapped, or fished themselves, or they bartered for it with their neighbors.

From the end of the Civil War to the beginning of the second World War, residents of the bayou country had more in common with each other, rich and poor, black and white, than they had with other people of their own class or race in other parts of the United States. Everyone spoke French. Almost everyone, in some way, was nourished by the land and water. Rich and poor alike were *vivant* and gregarious. They loved life and were out to enjoy it. They shared a fondness for food, drink, and celebration. They also shared a healthy contempt for the worlds of commerce and politics, considering them to be second-class ways to earn a living. They were Catholics and had large families.

The true Cajuns are descended from a group of French colonists who settled in Nova Scotia during the early seventeenth century. They called their new home Acadia. A century later, in 1713, the Treaty of Utrecht established English control over most of Nova Scotia. Life under English dominion grew increasingly difficult for the Acadians. An expulsion order was finally issued in 1755. The Acadians were rounded up and deported.

Their search for a new homeland was long and arduous. Many followed a "trail of tears" all the way to New Orleans. There, the French welcomed them and urged them to go out and settle the wet, nearly empty reaches of southern Louisiana along the Spanish Trail. There was plenty of land to go around and the Acadians were able to peacefully coexist with the small number of Spaniards who had already established themselves. The French word *Acadienne* was gradually Americanized to "a Cajun."

The Acadians, grateful for a place to settle and live in peace, rapidly adapted to the area's unique conditions. They farmed, fished, hunted, and trapped with consummate skill, and the bayous gave them ample room to practice these arts. They were self-sufficient people who continued, over the years, to zealously guard their self-sufficiency.

Southern Louisiana's rich traced their lineage back through the plantation owners whose ancestors had come directly to New Orleans from France in the eighteenth century and built an elegant, aristocratic society. Their labor force was composed of slaves and, later, free blacks, since the Cajuns were notoriously loath to work for wages on a regular basis. Creole is the name currently used to designate the descendants of Louisiana's European settlers, although the name was used in earlier centuries to mean a person of mixed racial or cultural background.

To be a black person in southern Louisiana was, and is, to be black in the deeply racist society of the Deep South. Slavery was a way of life before the Civil War. To this day, blacks are most often on the lowest rung of the employment ladder, and there are numerous obstacles thrown in the path of any black person who tries to rise above it. They are often relegated to doing menial and unskilled labor, and are the last hired and the first fired. As elsewhere in Dixie, it was the black people who worked the great landholdings, maintained the plantations, and nursed the infant landholders, but blacks were relentlessly denied any autonomy over their own lives.

Creole and Cajun alike maintained strong ties with the French culture through language, religion, and custom. Neither group had any use for the idea of local public schools. In fact, they were adamant about protecting their children from exposure to the cultural values of the rest of the United States. The Creoles sent their children to Paris to be educated. The Cajuns taught their progeny in boats, behind ploughs, and in the marshes.

It was with good reason that people in southern Louisiana were viewed as a breed apart. Until recently, the very word *Cajun* was considered to be an epithet, denoting a person who was shiftless, uneducated, and lazy. People from New Iberia might have used the word among themselves, but on the lips of a non-Cajun it would have been an insult, an ethnic slur, fighting words.

Albert Rhodes, a roving correspondent, wrote an article for a magazine called *The Galaxy* in 1873, in which he described American indignation over the Acadian approach to life: "He of Anglo-Saxon stock regards American civilization as the highest in the world, and insists that this Creole native shall square himself to it, but he persistently refuses—he prefers his own.

"Elsewhere the turning shop works successfully. The Indians are shaved down almost to annihilation; Mexicans of California and Texas assume the national shape; Alaskans are being cut down to the required model; and as for the Irish, they are hardly landed on the Battery before declarations are filed and they are turned out after the approved pattern. The Creole alone resists, and to the urgent demands of his Anglo-Saxon neighbor, his 'Non Monsieur,' comes back as unerringly as the refrain of Poe's raven."

Nevermore. Those days have passed. Now the dollar is king and the old ways are bygone ways. As early as 1922, education was made compulsory and the French language was banned in the classroom. A flamboyant populist from northern Louisiana named Huey Long was the state's governor from 1928 to 1936. During those eight years, he changed the face of the entire state by paving its roads. Until then, they had all been surfaced with dirt or clamshells.

Once the roads had been paved, anybody with four wheels could reach anyplace in the state where the ground was solid enough to hold a vehicle. Huey Long encouraged a steadily increasing development of Louisiana's onshore oil resources. A growing number of people found work in the oilfields during the 1930s, but the majority of Cajuns remained unaffected by this gradual expansion of the petroleum industry. Schools, roads, and onshore wells were early cracks in the fortress of tradition that isolated the Cajun culture, but the bedrock of their society remained secure until after the Second World War.

It was not until 1947, when the first offshore oil rig was sunk in the Gulf of Mexico forty-five miles southwest of Morgan City, that the borders of the bayou country were irrevocably breached. That first offshore rig is still standing today, along with over three thousand others spread out off the Gulf Coast. As the price of oil plunged in the mid-

1980s, some of the offshore wells were capped and their crews fired, but the corporations that owned them knew they had only to wait for the next boom cycle to come along, an event that would surely happen as long as the world depended on this finite resource for energy. Viewed in port, at the yards where they are built, the offshore oil rigs appear to be mammoth, towering steel structures of tanks, pipes, platforms, and catwalks; but seen from a distance, across the open Gulf, they appear delicate and vulnerable.

The arrogation and ownership of Acadiana's rich natural resources by outside interests was underway. The invasive force of late twentieth-century technology is strong, and the same process has been repeated in many different parts of the world. In some places, it has been industry that wedged a culture apart, and in others tourism has opened the door to cash flow and consumer values. Regardless of the method, the result is the same: people who have been self-sufficient for hundreds of years, and who have been their own bosses, are convinced to work for others in order to earn the money to buy things which they think they need and cannot provide for themselves.

Prior to the oil patch, outsiders who came to southern Louisiana looking for work, even such nearby neighbors as Texans, had to be willing to go into the fields. There was plenty of sugar cane and hot peppers that needed harvesting, but what else could a Texan have done? Would he have known how to make a living from a bayou or a marsh? Where to set traps for muskrats and crawfish? How to avoid water moccasins and alligators? The fishing boats that set out for oysters and shrimp certainly did not need any Texans for crew. There were plenty of family and friends who were glad for the work.

There are still people who trap and fish for a living, but they are becoming fewer and fewer, as are the numbers of small farmers still working this fertile region. Here, as all over the United States, the small farmer has almost disappeared. The economics of farming have become a continuous cycle of complicated credit arrangements and price supports, involving huge sums of money. Rice, soybeans, and sugar cane have become the crops of choice in Acadiana, and each gets farmed on a grand scale. Farms must be big in order to make money, and to be big they have to be mechanized; this creates an endless spiral of increasingly expensive machinery and vast tracts of land.

During the 1970s, in the face of intense competition from agribusiness, which made it increasingly difficult to make a profit, many small farmers in Iberia Parish found their land to be worth ten times as much as it had been ten years before. Not because of anything the land could produce, but because it was a piece of space in a growing outpost of the petroleum industry, and could be used for housing developments, trailer courts, or fast food restaurants.

The booming oil patch spelled disaster for the hot pepper crop, which depended on hand-harvesting. As industrial jobs opened up, people were no longer available to work in the fields. Louisiana led the nation in hot pepper production in 1938, with more than four thousand acres of peppers grown. By 1978, Louisiana had fallen behind all the southwestern states, and planted only a thousand acres in peppers, a decline of 75 percent over a forty-year period. By 1998, hot peppers had virtually disappeared, with less than 100 acres of them grown in the state.

Still, oil prosperity came relatively late to Iberia Parish, and when New Iberia's ship finally did come in, it did so at the Port of Iberia. The Port is seven miles south of New Iberia. It is barely connected to the Gulf, and fifty miles of Vermilion Bay have to be negotiated before reaching open water. The Port was a small-time operation supporting a dozen or so modest businesses until 1973, when funds were raised to deepen and widen the channel so that it could be used to handle larger ships and more traffic. After this was accomplished, drilling platforms could be constructed there and hauled across Vermilion Bay to the Gulf. New Iberia's Chamber of Commerce mounted an aggressive campaign to sell the Port to the petroleum industry. Their efforts were successful. Heavyweight companies like McDermott, Houston Systems, and PAR Industries located there. The Port became the parish's largest employer. In 1980, about $30 million in salaries were paid at the Port, and almost four thousand people were working there.

The Port, like much of the petroleum industry in southern Louisiana, depended not only on servicing and maintaining existing offshore wells, but also on exploration for new deposits. The construction of new rigs and the manufacture and sale of drilling equipment, pipes, and the machinery needed to explore for oil was a big part of the Port's business. When the petroleum market began to show signs of softening in 1981, and production (supply) outstripped demand, profits began to fall and exploration expenditures were among the first to be trimmed. From there, things got worse. McDermott, PAR, and Houston, the three largest industries at the Port, closed down. Employment at the Port sank below fifteen hundred people. Handwritten signs were nailed to the trees beside the road: Jesus Save Our Port. Whether it was Jesus, or a strengthening local and national economy, the Port did get saved. In 1998, there was, once again, full occupancy.

When I heard there was an old-fashioned Cajun night-spot in New Iberia where people still got together to drink, dance, and carouse, I went over on the first Saturday night that rolled around. It was a good thing, because after forty years of using the building as a dance hall the lumber company that owned it had decided to turn it into a warehouse. The night I went was the Blue Moon Club's last dance.

Even after forty years, the place looked like it would only take two people with crowbars about an hour to turn it into a warehouse. It was long, low, and dim, with a large rectangular wooden dance floor bordered with tables. The bar was against one wall. There was a crowd of people, young and old, some dressed up in coats and ties and others in blue jeans. Bottles of bourbon or cans of Dixie Beer graced almost every table. I stood at the bar and drank Jack Daniels, surrounded by conversations in French.

The small bandstand at the far end of the room was raised a foot or so off the floor. It was crowded with an accordion, an electric guitar, an electric bass, a fiddle, and trap drums. The drummer did most of the singing, often simply punctuating the music with a harmonious yodel or moan. Occasionally, the bartender left his post and stepped up to sing a song. All the lyrics were in French and had a strong country and western blues feeling to them. People two-stepped to the slow tunes and jitterbugged to the fast ones. The scene would have been much the same forty years before, except the band would have been made up of only a squeeze box, a fiddle, and a large triangle for percussion. Cajuns used to call these Saturday night get-togethers *fais-de-do*, a corruption of *fête de Dieu*, meaning festival of God.

I watched elderly women jitterbugging with each other, laughing and clapping. A thin, short man with his white hair brushed back, wearing cowboy boots and a string tie, spun his partner out to arm's length and pulled her back again. His boots moved fast, heels and toes popping on the worn wooden planks of the dance floor.

The band changed to a slow, plaintive lament. A bald man in a seersucker suit, wearing white socks and black loafers, two-stepped a lady with blond hair in a towering bouffant around the floor. When the music stopped, he escorted her back to their table, walking stiffly like an old man, but his dancing had been fluid and smooth.

Standing next to me at the bar was a man with short slate-gray hair and a rocky face that was stubbled and seamed. He was wearing faded blue overalls and had a broad-billed cap stuffed into his back pocket. He listened to a few tunes, drinking his Dixie from the can, watching the dance floor intently. Finally, he crossed to a table, found a partner, and began to two-step. He took his pleasure grimly, but with a certain grace.

Suddenly a fight erupted. My neighbor at the bar had apparently made an unwise decision about whom to ask for a dance, and he had been challenged with a shove by a younger, shorter man with broad arms and shoulders. They stepped outside to settle it and many followed to watch. Others kept dancing. The band played on, never missing a beat, as people spilled out the screen doors, down the wooden steps, and into the parking lot to form a circle around the combatants.

The fight was lit by a single bare bulb above the screen doors, and the faces of the crowd were in shadow. People maintained a respectful silence as the two men grunted and rolled around in the gravel. Moths slapped up against the lightbulb and fluttered, stunned, to the ground. The man standing next to me murmured, "It's a good thing they don't be usin' knives. I've seen that plenny of times, me. It's not Saturday night without a fight. This'll be over in no time. Too bad. I like to see a good fight."

He was right. The fight ended in a couple of minutes. The older man took the worst of it, and his left eye was swollen almost shut. His assailant had suffered a bloody nose, so both were satisfied. They drifted back inside with the crowd to have another drink and a few more dances. So did I.

The bartender spoke of plans to reopen the Blue Moon at a different location. But rents were high, *cher*, and the right spot was yet to be found. Even so, it was clear from the diversity and exuberance of the club's patrons that the tradition of getting together to drink and dance was not in immediate danger of disappearing. I was told that within a ten-parish radius of New Iberia there were thirty-one makers of Cajun accordions. Instruments and songs were still handed down from generation to generation, and there was no shortage of performers, two-steppers, or jitterbuggers. When I left at one in the morning, things were still going strong, and the band was swinging into an up-tempo version of *Ma Jolie Blonde*.

he tabasco pepper is a small, thin-walled pepper, rarely exceeding two and a half inches in length. As a rule, the smaller a pepper, the hotter it is. The hottest peppers in the world are all less than three inches long. Many of them belong to the species *Capsicum frutescens*, but tabasco peppers are the only variety of this species that grows in the United States, and it is believed to have been introduced to Louisiana by Edmund McIlhenny, the first McIlhenny to make Tabasco Sauce. All the other peppers cultivated north of Mexico—cayennes, jalapeños, anchos, chilies, even bells—are varieties of *Capsicum annuum* (pronounced *ann-you-um*).

If peppers are rated on a heat scale of one to ten, tabasco merits an eight. No *annuum* can compare with it in pungency, but the tabasco pepper is hard to farm. Difficult to grow and painful to pick, it is, nevertheless, the quintessential Louisiana hot pepper.

Tabascos were the pepper around which Edmund McIlhenny, in 1868, and B. F. Trappey, in 1898, began their respective hot sauce businesses. For over one hundred years, the McIlhenny Company marketed only one product, Tabasco Sauce, while B. F. Trappey and Sons diversified to the point of marketing over fifty food products in the United States and abroad. Trappey was the world's leading producer of canned yams and also marketed a variety of bean products. In addition to a line of standard hot sauces, it manufactured a number of specialty items like Green Dragon Whole Jalapeño Peppers and Serrano Brand Hot Pickled Peppers.

International headquarters for the Trappey Company was a modest, low office building on East Main Street in New Iberia. I arrived early for my appointment with W. J. Trappey, president of the company. I shared the comfortable waiting room with two salesmen who were dressed in suits, each with a large sample case resting between black, well-polished wingtip shoes. Next to each vinyl chair was a small table with a telephone on it.

The older salesman placed a credit card call to Jackson, Mississippi, and reserved a room for the following night. The younger man used his credit card number to call his home office in Atlanta and file a brief report on how things had gone in Baton Rouge. I could not determine exactly what it was that either man was selling, but it was evident that there were plenty of people between the person who grew the hot peppers and the person who ate them: legions of drummers, home offices, food brokers, and supermarket personnel.

W. J. Trappey came out to the waiting room and led me back to his office. He was a short, portly, balding man. On one wall of his paneled office was a stuffed tarpon. He reached into a desk drawer and pulled out a tiny bottle of hot sauce, which he placed on his desk top. He leaned back in his swivel chair and his feet swung momentarily free of the floor. He regarded the bottle as if it were an antique of inestimable value.

"My grandfather started this business in 1898, with that hot sauce right there," he said. "At that time, of course, he was growing his own peppers. We haven't grown our own peppers in a long time, but until recently we bought all of them from Louisiana farmers. Presently, only 5 percent of what we buy is grown here in the state. Now we have to go to Texas, around the Rio Grande valley. We also get a little out of Mexico. Every year we buy 3 or 4 million pounds of peppers, and we have had to begin using big growers who produce a hundred acres for us, instead of fifty farmers who grow two acres apiece."

The hot sauce business had never been better, according to Trappey. "There's more interest in hot peppers in the last ten years than ever before. If you become accustomed to them, things just don't taste right without them. If someone starts right, just using a little until they build up their taste, it's just a natural thing to like peppers. People who start using them correctly want to use more and more as time goes on. Hot sauce is selling well now in the North and Midwest, places where they never ate hot food before."

The brand of hot sauce that the Trappey Company marketed, varied from place to place. "In San Francisco, they took a fancy to Red Devil and that's the brand we sell there. When you get down to Los Angeles, or up your way to Portland, our brand is Mexi-Pep. The one called Louisiana Hot Sauce is our most price-competitive product. It's made from peppers we would reject for our better brands. Yet I have people from the Midwest who write and tell me that it's the best damned hot sauce they have ever eaten."

Despite the fact that W. J. Trappey expressed satisfaction about the sales of hot sauces in 1978, the company was experiencing difficulties. The sons referred to in the company name numbered seven, all of them in some way connected to the company, and the business had become too spread out, according to observers. In 1981, dismayed by a lack of profits, the stockholders decided to make some changes. A chief executive officer, Jack Blenderman, was brought in from outside the family, and a major housecleaning took place. By 1986, the only Trappey still active in the business was 91-year-old Bernard, who was chairman of the board.

Jack Blenderman was not much of a hot sauce user, far from addicted to the stuff, but he was a good manager, and he made a number of changes that worked to make the company more competitive in both the domestic and international hot sauce markets. A radical belt-tightening took place throughout the company. The phones disappeared from the lobby, 150 employees disappeared from the payroll, and a number of members of the Trappey family took early retirement. It was not enough, however. In 1991, the company's hot sauce division was sold to its old competitor, the McIlhenny Company. It did not turn out to be a good fit, however, and in June 1997 the makers of Tabasco Sauce sold Trappey's to a New Jersey food products company.

Cayennes and jalapeños are the basic peppers in most of Trappey's hot sauces. Although these *annuum* are not as hot as tabascos, they are hot enough to satisfy the average American palate, and they can be grown in southern Texas with ease. They do not burn a picker's hands like tabascos, and there is a large reservoir of Mexican labor around the Rio Grande valley. Seventy-five percent of the peppers used by the company to make its hot sauces and pepper products are grown in Texas and New Mexico, and the remainder are from Honduras, Mexico, and the Dominican Republic. The Trappeys market only one brand of hot sauce that is still manufactured entirely from tabasco peppers. It is called simply Trappey's Pepper Sauce, and is sold mostly in southern Louisiana.

The manufacture of any hot sauce worth its name begins with a mash of crushed peppers. This is aged for at least two years. When the weather is warm, the mash will "work," meaning it bubbles and gives off gas. Since neither alcohol nor sugar is produced during this process, it is not fermentation. It is believed that the weight of the mash on the crushed peppers releases carbon dioxide trapped in the pepper tissue. This gas, rising to the surface, causes the mash to bubble. By the third year of aging, the mash stops working and is ready to be bottled. The aging process breaks down the fiber-cellular bundles in the mash and releases the oils from the peppers. Viewed under a microscope, a good hot sauce is an almost pure emulsion of oil and vinegar.

There are three general categories of hot sauce on the market. The lowest quality is made by manufacturers who cut corners by using twentieth-century food technology. No one in Acadiana makes hot sauce this way, but it is done. At a terrible sacrifice of flavor, manufacturers of rot-gut hot sauce use dehydrated peppers, xanthin gums, coal-tar colors, and other wonders developed by the modern food industry. The aging process, of course, goes by the boards.

The next step up in the hierarchy of hot sauce is what W. J. Trappey called "price competitive." These are sauces that have been properly aged, with no industrial additives. The whole pepper, usually a cayenne or a jalapeño, is ground up very fine—seeds, husks, and all—and used in the hot sauce. This is the *vin ordinaire*, a decent product at an affordable price.

The highest quality and most expensive hot sauces have had the seeds and husks pulped out after the mash has aged. This yields an exceptionally rich, red, heavy product. The discriminating hot sauce devotee will insist that the time and effort required for this process can be justified only when *Capsicum frutescens* is used.

Hot sauces are more than just hot. Different varieties of peppers make sauces with flavors that range from exciting and full-bodied to dull and thin. As with wines, the quality of the original fruit will, to a large extent, determine the quality of the finished product. There is no question that tabasco peppers provide a treat for the discerning taste which cannot be found among the *annuum*.

W. J. Trappey told me regretfully, "We just don't use much tabasco, anymore. The little that we do need is grown for us here in Louisiana. It's a hell of a tough pepper to grow. Sometimes you don't get a bush. Sometimes you'll have a bush and no fruit. Sometimes you'll get a beautiful bush with a lot of fruit, and it won't have any damned seed. Tabasco will not grow commercially in many places. It will do well here, although it may grow in one spot and ten miles away it just won't do right, no matter how hard you try."

One place where tabasco peppers consistently do right is on Avery Island, home of the McIlhenny Company. The first tabasco peppers to be grown in this country were cultivated on Avery Island by a McIlhenny before the Civil War, and the island still produces more tabascos than anywhere else in the United States.

Avery Island is not really an island. It is a huge dome of rock salt, three miles long, and two and a half miles wide, located seven miles south of New Iberia, surrounded by wet marsh and the Bayou Petit Anse. The great hill of salt was forced up by movement deep in the earth, pushing the ground above it. Dig down thirteen feet through the island's soil cover and you strike salt.

There is so much of it that the International Salt Company, which has leased a mine on the southern end of the island since 1899, has been able to remove millions of tons and barely tap the surface of the vast deposit of 99 percent pure salt. Furthermore, oil is usually found close to such domes, and Avery Island is no exception. Humble Oil Company, later to become Exxon USA, struck black gold there in 1941.

By 1986, the field had produced about 95 million barrels, which made it Exxon's largest onshore oil field in southern Louisiana. The McIlhennys have insisted on protecting the island's flora and fauna in their leasing arrangements with oil companies through the years—all pipes are underground, for instance—and Exxon's current presence on the island is barely visible.

Tabasco peppers thrive in the oily, salty soil. For nearly a hundred years, all the peppers used to make Tabasco Sauce were grown on Avery Island. This would still be the case if it had not been for a chronic shortage of pepper pickers in Iberia Parish. In 1985, the company sold about 70 million bottles of hot sauce, but only about 2 percent of the peppers they turned into mash that year were grown on Avery Island. The rest were farmed in Mexico, Honduras, Colombia, and Venezuela—places where labor is cheap and plentiful, and where *Capsicum frutescens* grows as well as it does on Avery Island.

Picking tabasco peppers is hard work. Some people would call it plain brutal. The pickers do not wear gloves. The peppers are small and must be picked carefully or they will break. They burn the flesh, although they do not raise a blister. As pickers get used to the work, they learn not to wipe any stray drops of sweat out of their eyes. Handling a tabasco pepper, then touching an eye, is guaranteed to produce a few minutes of painful blindness. It passes.

The McIlhenny Company raised the price for picked peppers from ten to twenty cents a pound in the late 1960s. In 1978 they raised it again, to thirty cents a pound. By 1986 it was up to thirty-three cents a pound. An average, steady picker could harvest sixty to eighty pounds per day and earn close to twenty dollars. That was not enough to bring many people to the fields looking for work. After the oil boom went bust, some working-age men began to return to the pepper fields for the harvest, but for most it was a last resort, something to be done only after unemployment benefits had run out and there was no other way to put food on the table. By 1998, with the unemployment rate low, the company had raised the price per pound to sixty cents, but they could draw no more than an average of thirty pickers to the fields each day.

Pickers, for the most part, have always been black. As black people gained more access to education, there were fewer who were willing to come out to the pepper fields. Even before Iberia Parish's oil prosperity of the 1970s, the number of people willing to pick peppers from August to November was dwindling. No one wants to perform the hot, monotonous, painful labor of picking tabasco peppers when anything else is available.

Faced with a vanishing labor pool in the middle 1970s, the company explored its options. It came up with only two, and decided to pursue both. The first was to hire a representative to work in Central and South America, someone fluent in Spanish who could determine where tabascos would grow well, then contract with farmers in those places to produce the peppers. In 1976, the company hired Gene Jefferies, a man with a master's degree in agricultural economics and twelve years of experience working on agricultural development projects in South America. The choice of Jefferies proved to be an excellent one.

The second option pursued by the company was to invest in research aimed at developing a mechanical pepper harvester. The first attempts were made by trying to adapt the existing technology to the pepper crop. Both green bean and blueberry harvesters were considered, tried, and discarded. During the 1970s, there were a number of people in universities and private engineering firms who were trying to design a pepper harvester, but it was not easy.

The primary difficulty was that hot peppers ripen at different times on the same bush. In the case of tabascos in southern Louisiana, for instance, from the end of July until the first frost, around the end of November, there will constantly be some red, ripe peppers and some immature green ones on every bush. A mechanical harvester, on any given pass, must pick only the ripe peppers. If too many immature peppers are knocked from the bush, or the bush is damaged, money is lost.

There are only so many ways mechanically to dislodge a pepper from a bush. Most efforts concentrated on either shaking the bush violently enough to dislodge the peppers or spraying them hard with jets of water. In both cases, the trick was to knock the reds onto a conveyor belt while leaving the green fruit attached and the bush alive.

It turned out that although it is easier to dislodge a ripe pepper from a bush than a green one, the amount of force required varies from bush to bush. Human pickers adapted by touch, but a machine needed to be stopped and adjusted. During the time it took to stop, fiddle, test, and reset to the proper water pressure or vibration level, a human picker would keep plodding along, picking what was ripe, leaving what was not. The human senses were hard to replicate.

A pair of experimental mechanical harvesters built in New Iberia were almost profitable—but not quite. The prototype Mark One harvester, built for the McIlhenny Company by Herman Schellstede and Associates of New Iberia, picked over eight thousand pounds of tabasco peppers on its best day, which is the work of a hundred good pickers. However, there were many days when it was hampered by mechanical problems and never picked a row.

The prototype Mark Two, which saw action during the harvest season of 1977, picked an average of 882 pounds a day. Good, but not good enough. The company needed a machine that would consistently do the work of a hundred people, not ten or fifteen.

The tomato, another member of the *Solanaceae* family, affords an example of the way in which mechanization is applied to a fruit. The tomato industry developed a mechanical harvester. While engineers designed the machine, agricultural botanists bred a tough-skinned tomato that would not be bruised by a harvester. Chemical engineers found that by spraying a green tomato with a chemical called ethrel while it was still on the bush, premature ripening could be induced. As a result of all these efforts, the old garden variety of tomato has disappeared from grocery shelves and has been replaced with something that can be harvested mechanically but that has considerably less taste, texture, and tomato-ness.

The replacement of human labor with mechanical harvesters usually means breeding plants for quantity instead of quality and replacing the natural ripening process with a chemical forgery. These sorts of breeding experiments were also being done on hot peppers. Much of that kind of work was carried on by academicians, under grants from private sectors of the pepper industry. As in many university departments, the money to support research and acquire equipment was there only when that research and equipment would serve business or government.

In the mid-1970s, it was discovered that ethrel would ripen peppers on the bush in the same way it did tomatoes, and it was put to use in certain California pepper fields. Concurrent ripening of all the peppers on a bush made harvesting much more economical, but the McIlhenny Company refused even to experiment with the use of ethrel on their crop. An ethrel-ripened pepper is still hot, since the capsaicin is already present in the immature peppers, but the McIlhennys were positive it would not have the flavor and juiciness of the sun-ripened item.

The company was convinced that it was this sort of concern about quality that had made Tabasco Sauce the best-known hot sauce in the world. The McIlhennys have insisted on paying close attention to detail and adhering to their traditional methods of doing things. They can well afford to do so. It is not every family that rests its fortunes on such a solid foundation as oil, salt, and peppers.

The seven miles of road between New Iberia and Avery Island ran beside flat marshland, which was dotted with cattails, stiff rushes, and marsh grasses. Herons flew over, or swooped down to stand poised on delicate stalk legs, unmoving, completely alert to their hunt. Red-winged blackbirds swayed back and forth on the tops of the cattails. There was an occasional patch of solid ground, often holding a small house raised on a foundation of the ubiquitous cement blocks.

The highest piece of ground in the entire state of Louisiana is only 535 feet above sea level, so Avery Island at 158 feet made a prominent mound as I approached it across the marsh from New Iberia. The road crossed a bridge over the Bayou Petit Anse and ran into a stop sign beside a gatehouse.

A middle-aged man came out, took my name, and telephoned to confirm that I had an appointment with Walter Stauffer McIlhenny, president of the company. Reassured, the guard came back and gave me directions.

I drove down the narrow road. On my right was a dense wall of high bamboo and on my left were a number of oil wells rhythmically pumping in a distant field. I turned left across a railroad track and parked, as instructed, by an old, ivy-covered brick building. This was the factory in which the aged pepper mash was turned into Tabasco Sauce. The very air was full of the concentrated odor of hot sauce. My sinuses tingled.

The company offices were in an elegant two-story building. The first-floor foyer, hung with a gleaming chandelier, was the waiting room. Behind the walls that flanked it were offices filled with secretaries, bookkeepers, typewriters, and telephones.

At the far end of the foyer was a winding staircase with a dark, polished banister, which led to the second floor, where members of the McIlhenny family had their offices. The largest of these second-floor offices belonged to Walter McIlhenny. Just outside its double doors stood a life-sized cardboard figure of a Marine in full-dress uniform, the sort of thing usually found in front of recruiting offices.

Walter McIlhenny was in his late sixties. He had the large, ruddy face characteristic of men in his family. His white hair was cut short and he had a bushy walrus mustache. When he read, he wore a pair of gold-rimmed, half-lens spectacles over his brown eyes. He had served as a Marine Corps battalion commander in the Pacific during World War II, and he was a strong supporter of the Corps during his entire life. He had been president of the McIlhenny Company for over thirty years and was a lifelong bachelor.

Walter McIlhenny evoked a strong sense of southern gentility. He maintained a dignified reserve and distance. The avocations he pursued during his life were the gentlemanly pleasures: he bred champion field dogs, which were boarded and cared for off the island; he went abroad on hunting safaris; and he was at one time considered to be among the best marksmen in the United States. Age had compacted and stooped what had once been a powerful frame, but when I visited him in 1978, he was still riding horseback for an hour in the evenings when the weather was good.

He spoke in mellifluous, gravelly tones, and his voice took on a deeper timbre as he narrated the history of his family and Tabasco Sauce. He told the tale with pleasure, choosing his words carefully, and paused often to wait for just the right word to come to mind. Like many a military man, he professed great admiration for accurately written history, and considered the American historian Samuel

Eliot Morison to be one of the greatest writers of our time. Once every fifteen minutes, a polished brass ship's clock behind his broad desk chimed the quarter-hour in a single silver tone.

"In the early 1850s, a soldier returning to New Orleans from Mexico gave my grandfather, Edmund McIlhenny, a dozen or so dried peppers, and told him to try them in his food. He used one or two and liked it, so he saved the seeds from the remaining peppers and planted them. He grew them in his wife's garden at Avery Island. He had married Mary Eliza Avery, the daughter of Judge Daniel Dudley Avery.

"The Civil War came along and there was no money to buy seasonings or anything else. They had to make do with what was at hand. We had salt here, so you could put salt in your food. Catch fish, shoot deer, raise potatoes, but you couldn't buy anything. My grandfather took some of the peppers which were growing in the garden and tried drying them. Then he tried pickling them with salt. Finally, he came up with a method of making a sauce.

"During the Civil War, salt was a real problem for the Confederacy. They needed it to preserve their meat and they couldn't get enough of it. They were collecting salt by going into the smokehouses and taking the drippings from the sides of pigs and beef, using the dirt that absorbed those drippings and mixing it with water to put on the meat."

In 1862, Judge Avery gave each of the southern states the chance to scrape and quarry Avery Island salt for a reasonable fee. A causeway of planks was built to the saltworks. Wagonloads of the precious mineral rolled toward Confederate lines. Ten thousand tons of salt were removed in eleven months, but in April 1863, the Union Army arrived at Avery Island, determined to put an end to this traffic. The Averys and the McIlhennys left Louisiana with a group of war refugees and waited in Texas for the cessation of hostilities.

When the family returned, they found much of the island had been destroyed along with the saltworks. The plantation was a shambles. Judge Avery was said to have been holding $3 million in worthless Confederate currency that had been paid for his salt. The times were full of turmoil, confusion, and loss.

However, some of the pepper bushes had survived the Union pillage, and Edmund McIlhenny began experimenting with a new batch of hot sauce. He passed some on to a General Hazard, who was the federal administrator in the region. The general knew a good thing when he tasted it, and his brother happened to be the largest whole-sale grocer in the United States. General Hazard sent some of the hot sauce to his brother in New York, and told him that it was made from a new kind of chili pepper. On the strength of the purchase orders that followed, Edmund McIlhenny began a commercial operation in 1868.

Edmund McIlhenny is thought to have named his sauce after the region of Mexico through which the Tabasco River runs, which is currently the state of Tabasco. "When my grandfather first put his sauce on the market, he called it McIlhenny Sauce," Walter McIlhenny told me. "That wasn't very inspiring. He wanted to name it for the plantation, but Judge Avery was of the old school and didn't want his name used in commerce. In my grandfather's diary, we find that he considered a number of different names. One of them was Tabasco . . . Pepper Sauce. Not tabasco pepper . . . sauce. You see? He was naming the sauce, not the pepper.

"He then sold his product for twenty years. In 1888, two botanists in Geneva, New York, Drs. Irish and Sturtevant, became aware of a *Capsicum* that had never identified or classified. They described the *Capsicum frutescens*, and in their notes on the specimen they christened it tabasco, because it was the pepper, 'used by Mister McIlhenny in New Iberia in the manufacture of his well-known Tabasco Sauce.' "

When Edmund McIlhenny died in 1890, his eldest son John, Walter's father, took over the company. In 1906, John moved his family to Washington, D.C., and Edward Avery McIlhenny, Edmund's second son, assumed the presidency, a position he was to hold for more than forty years. He was known to almost every man, woman, and child in Iberia Parish as Mister Ned, or M'sieu Ned, and was accorded great respect. He had a deservedly wide reputation as a botanist, naturalist, and writer, and is often referred to as the father of conservation efforts in Louisiana. He was instrumental in having over 164,000 acres of southern Louisiana's marshlands set aside as a wildlife refuge.

M'sieu Ned was an avid ornithologist, who personally banded nearly twenty thousand birds during his lifetime. Bird-lovers the world over still link his name with the snowy egret, which he saved from virtual extinction. In the spring of 1892, the nuptial plumage of the snowy egret constituted the highest fashion. Every stylish lady was crowned with a hat bearing one of the beautiful white plumes. Designers in Europe and the United States clamored for them.

The nuptial plumage appears only during the egret's nesting season in the spring. The birds traditionally returned from their winters in South America to nest in the marshes of southern Louisiana, particularly around Iberia Parish. They made ridiculously easy targets as they sat on their nests. The population was decimated in no time and the value of the plumage continued to rise as the bird grew scarcer.

M'sieu Ned tried to get some action from the Louisiana state legislature, but it was not forthcoming. He was only twenty in 1892, and his lobbying skills were not as good as they would be in his later years. By late spring, he could not find a single live egret around Avery Island. Ned recruited two company employees and went into the marsh. They spent three days slogging through it, finding nothing but dead egrets beside their nests, intact save for a bullet hole and a few missing plumes. The chicks that had hatched before their mothers were killed had starved. On the third day, deep in the marsh, they found two nests containing a total of seven live chicks.

A pond was constructed at Avery Island, and a large platform placed in its center. A cage was built on the platform with ample room for the chicks to fly as they matured. The following spring, in 1893, the birds selected mates among themselves, built nests, and hatched young. No wild egrets were seen in the marshes that year. The approach of autumn signaled the time when the birds would normally migrate. Ned McIlhenny destroyed the cage and the birds flew south. In the spring of 1894, his hopes were rewarded when the birds returned to nest on the platform. Those seven chicks were the ancestors of a colony of snowy egrets which currently numbers a hundred thousand at the height of nesting season.

In later years, Ned McIlhenny surrounded his bird refuge with 250 acres of the vast botanical collection that he had amassed during his lifetime. He named this part of the island The Jungle Gardens. Among the specimens that grow there are over eight hundred varieties of camellias, sixty-four varieties of bamboo, thirty thousand azalea bushes, and lotus flowers from the upper Nile. Each year, more than fifty thousand tourists visit these gardens.

Another reason Ned McIlhenny will be remembered for a long time in Louisiana is that he introduced the nutria to the state. This is a furry rodent, which looks like a huge rat. He imported quite a few pair from South America and kept them under observation for several years. A hurricane came through, wrecked his fences, and the nutria escaped into the surrounding marsh. They are prolific breeders. A litter born in January is producing young by the end of the year. Nutria have their teats on their backs, and the fur on their bellies has considerable value in the fur market.

Ned McIlhenny had hoped the nutria would thrive on the water hyacinths that frequently clog Louisiana's waterways, and thus keep the bayous clear while they kept themselves fed. Unfortunately, the nutria were just as glad to settle for a diet of garden crops. Citizens in the parishes around Avery Island grew increasingly irate as they watched the nutria proliferate and attack their gardens. The animal was eventually accorded official state recognition as a nuisance. As the price of fur began to climb, however, attitudes toward the nutria began to change. In 1968, it was removed from Louisiana's list of undesirable animals. Nutria pelts were selling for about eight dollars apiece in 1977, and brought almost $15 million into the state. The pelts dyed well and were on a par with mink and beaver.

In 1940, thirty-year-old Walter McIlhenny was summoned to Avery Island from his home in Virginia by his Uncle Ned. He began working for the company and being groomed for its presidency. Ned had fathered three daughters and no sons. He wanted a man at the company's helm. Walter left Avery Island to serve with the Marines during the war, but returned after the Allied victory.

In 1949, upon Ned McIlhenny's death, Walter succeeded to the presidency of the company. In the same year, twenty-two-year-old Ned Simmons, son of M'sieu Ned's daughter Polly McIlhenny Simmons, joined the company. Walter McIlhenny died in 1985 of Parkinson's Disease, and Ned Simmons assumed the presidency. His two younger cousins, Edmund and Paul McIlhenny, were named as vice-presidents.

The company's shareholders and board of directors are all members of the McIlhenny family. But when the hot sauce market began to take off in the late 1980s and early 1990s, they felt that the company's profits were not keeping pace with the market, and they decided to bring in an outsider who could meld marketing and management.

The man chosen was Vince Pierce, a New York native who was the company's Asian director. He was tapped in 1996, but two years later he was gone, asked by the board to resign, and Paul McIlhenny was named president in his place. Even though the outside-the-family experiment did not last long, Pierce changed the face of the company during his brief tenure.

"We make one product and we make it well," Walter McIlhenny had told me in 1978, but by 1998 the company was making a wide range of food products, including a pepper garlic sauce, a chili con carne sauce, and a habanero pepper sauce. Furthermore, they were producing a mail-order catalogue featuring hundreds of Tabasco brand products, including clothing, watches, and sports equipment, and they had laid out more than $1 million to sponsor a NASCAR driver and have their logo on his car.

When Walter McIlhenny spoke to me in 1978 about the things that had occurred during his tenure as president, he spoke with pride of increased production and the expansion of the market for Tabasco Sauce. Since he had taken over in 1949, the company had gone from a self-contained seigneury to a modern, thriving business. Nevertheless, there occasionally crept into his voice a note of the same wistfulness that had characterized Stella Larson's eulogy of the old days.

"We used to have two, three, four hundred people a day harvesting in the fields this time of the year," he said. "Today we've got sixty or seventy out there. We can no longer get them and we've been forced to move a great deal of our agricultural activity to where there are people who still desire this kind of work."

He suggested I see some Avery Island tradition at work, and used the phone to summon Edmund McIlhenny into the office. He asked Edmund to take me along for the weighing of the day's harvest. Walter himself had ritually performed this task every afternoon for twenty-five harvest seasons, but with his health not at its best he delegated it to his younger relatives. He solemnly assured me that I was about to witness the manner in which pepper pickers on Avery Island had been paid for their day's labor, "since beyond any living memory."

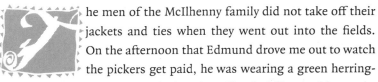he men of the McIlhenny family did not take off their jackets and ties when they went out into the fields. On the afternoon that Edmund drove me out to watch the pickers get paid, he was wearing a green herringbone tweed jacket and a dark tie. The office building had been air-conditioned and cool, but outside it was over eighty degrees.

Edmund had the ruddy face and light brown hair of his family. He looked, in fact, remarkably like his namesake, the company's founder, in a surviving portrait from the 1850s. Edmund was thirty-four years old. He was born and raised in New Orleans, and graduated from Tulane Law School. He interned in Washington, D.C., with Senator Joe Clark of Pennsylvania, then returned to New Orleans where he practiced law. He had been living on Avery Island with his wife and two children since 1975. He did not seem to miss city life and described himself, with a chuckle, as a retired member of the Louisiana State Bar.

We were riding in one of the McIlhenny's fleet of blue, late-model American sedans. The road was gravel and we left a cloud of dust in the air behind us. In 1910, the pepper fields came right up to the walls of the old factory, but they have receded, and it took a ten-minute ride along the narrow island road to reach them. During the harvest season, old school buses came into New Iberia from Avery Island at 5:30 every morning but Sunday to give the pickers a ride out to the pepper fields. There was an hour for a meal in the middle of the day, and the work stopped at 3:45 P.M.

Edmund and I arrived at the fields shortly after four o'clock. Thirteen acres of tabasco peppers were coming ripe under the bright afternoon sun. Pepper bushes three feet high were loaded with red and green erect pods as far as the eye could see. A dirt road, called the headland, ran down one side of each field along the ends of the rows. The pickers were beside the headland, sitting on overturned buckets or on the ground, with boxes of scarlet peppers around them. The boxes looked as old as any of the traditions in force on Avery Island. They were wooden, two feet long and a foot deep, sturdy and worn. Each weighed eight pounds when empty.

The pickers were all black, almost all women over forty-five. There were a handful of young women and a few old men. There was not a young man in sight. The women wore bonnets or kerchiefs. The sun-bleached reds and blues of their headgear bobbed and flashed in the hot dusty air as they patiently waited for the weighing of the day's work to begin.

I had a moment's impression of peace and well-being, compounded from the smell of the warm soil and the sight of people resting beside their harvests. It disappeared as I focused on the pickers, the sweat cooling on their faces, the exhaustion in their eyes, the bone-tired postures into which their bodies had settled. During the summer months and on Saturdays during the fall, black high school students, boys and girls, often came out to pick. Their supply of energy was unlimited and they shouted, chattered, and horsed around during the midday meal or while waiting for the McIlhennys to begin weighing. But it was a weekday; most of the pickers had gray hair. Their fatigue was palpable.

All eyes were on Edmund and me as we got out of the car and walked down the headland. At the far end were two trucks and a number of men dressed in the tan uniforms of McIlhenny Company employees. Edmund exchanged greetings with the pickers as we walked by them, speaking to many by name.

When we reached the trucks at the bottom of the headland, I noticed a two-wheeled cart attached by a trailer hitch to the first truck. A large platform scale was mounted on the cart. Paul McIlhenny was waiting for us beside it. He and Edmund were first cousins of nearly the same age, and they bore a strong resemblance to each other. Paul was dressed in a blazer, gray flannels, and a dark tie. There was a bit of banter between them about who would weigh and who would pay, until Paul conceded that it was his turn to weigh. He climbed into the cart and sat down beside the scales on a little three-legged milking stool.

The truck pulled the cart slowly up the headland, stopping at each picker and box of peppers. One of the company men walked in front of the truck and poked a stick down through the peppers in the boxes to make sure the picker had not loaded them with rocks in the bottom. When the truck stopped, a company man would lift a box onto the scale. Paul adjusted the weight on the scale's beam and solemnly called out the number of pounds. The box was removed and stacked on the second truck, which was following behind. Paul seemed slightly ill at ease and out of place, perched in the cart on the low stool, thumbing the scale.

The truck lurched forward and stopped every few feet so a box could be hoisted up to the scale. I watched as Paul weighed a box. The woman who had picked that box of peppers stood on the ground, gazing up toward his flushed, sweaty face, her eyes stopping somewhere around the knot in his tie as he fiddled with the weights.

"Sixty-five," he called out. An employee inside the truck recorded the weight, subtracting eight pounds for the box, and punched it on a card.

The woman was at least fifty, and she had spent her day picking those fifty-seven pounds of peppers. She smiled, her face streaked with sweat under her red bonnet. "How y'all doin', Mistah Paul?"

"Fine thanks, Miss Rose. Made yourself a little money today, I guess. Gonna see you tomorrow, aren't we?"

She laughed. "Course you will, Mistah Paul. If I ain't out here, you know my health done give out. You jist know I be done for if I ain't here."

She took her punched card from a hand waving it out the window of the truck's cab and walked up the headland to Edmund McIlhenny, who stood by another late-model sedan. This one had an open cash box on the hood. Edmund took her punched card, wrote down her name and how much she had picked in a large ledger, and counted $16.10 into her palm. Miss Rose received it in silence, signed her X in the ledger beside her name, and climbed wearily aboard the school bus to wait for her ride back to New Iberia.

The school buses were painted olive green and had "The McIlhenny Company" printed on their sides. By the time everyone had been paid in the traditional manner and the bus had rattled its slow way back to New Iberia, it would already be five o'clock, with barely enough time left for these women to start getting supper on the stove once they got home.

*

While the truck pulled Paul slowly up the headland, I spoke with Willie Doré, the field foreman at Avery Island. He was in his middle forties. French was his first language and he spoke English with a thick, Cajun accent. To my ears, the English spoken in southern Louisiana is second only to that spoken in the Caribbean in the loveliness of its tones. Words seem to roll off the tongue, making softer and less harsh sounds than English spoken elsewhere. No matter if the conversation is only about the weather or last night's television show, the song of the spoken words makes them sound like poetry.

Willie Doré was wearing a white shirt, open at the collar, and a broad-brimmed hat. He had light, freckled skin and the hat kept him shaded. People here, as in many white, rural societies around the world, regard the lightest, whitest skin as the most desirable. Despite the subtropical heat, they do not like to go under the hot sun with bare arms or uncovered heads. They are baffled by city folks who lie exposed beneath blazing rays in order to turn darker.

Willie was grateful for the security offered him by the McIlhenny Company. He was a loyal and devoted employee. "I was born on Avery Island. When my daddy and family left I was five years old, and when we came back I was nineteen. I been here ever since. My daddy had worked here about ten years, and then went to share farming. But there wasn't no money in it, and we wanted to come to work where they paid every week and at least you could see money. Farming, you wouldn't see it until the end of the year, and then just maybe you'd see some. So when we got back here I just stayed on."

He shook his head sadly. "There were about fifty or sixty out here pickin' today. I got work for a hunnerd and twenny. See that ole lady who's weighin' out now? She's been pickin' over fifty years. Strong and healthy like an ole mule, cher. Still be the same people pickin'. I believe after these people die, nobody be comin' out a-tall. They need to find a good machine, but Lord, this one they got now be just a bit better than nothin'. It's slow and the machine gotta use so much pressure it always be knockin' the greens off the bush."

Willie Doré has been growing tabasco peppers for a long time. Like any farmer, he could remember some good years and some bad ones, but he could not remember a season when everything went right. "The ideal weather for peppers to grow in would be a half inch of rain every week, and then sunshine. Clouds now and then, a little clouds, but I'm talkin' the ideal. If you have sunshine, it's all right, but if it be cloudy it's better, 'cause your moisture stays. If your wind goes south your moisture comes up, if it goes north then it comes down. The last couple of days we had that wind from the north, and right now the rows be dry, dry, dry. That stops the crop from growing right there. Oh yes, cher, that completely stop it.

"This year we was late gettin' started 'cause we had cold nights for the longest time. Lord, we not usually seein' that many cold nights. Your pepper plant likes to grow at night, in the warm night air. We put 'em out this year in April, but at night it was real cold, right in the fifties for a long time. Usually these nights be much warmer and we start pickin' in the last week of July, but this year we didn't get goin' until the middle of August.

"So that be three weeks we was late gettin' started with our pickin'. You losin' that, plus you losin' the time when you able to get the kids to come out and pick. This is why we always strain so much to have a good start, so we can have the kids for a month before they go back to school. That's when we make our good pickin'. After they be back in school, we not gettin' much in the way of hand-pickers, but when the kids are pickin', you can get a hunnerd and twenny people out here."

By 1986, things had changed. The McIlhennys were purposely waiting until school resumed to begin picking Avery Island peppers, so that they would not have to fool with adolescents and their horseplay. There was plenty of available adult labor—deadly serious about the work—and it did not pay to have kids out there picking only half a box a day.

When the oil patch slowed down in 1981 and the first wave of laid-off workers came to the end of their unemployment benefits a year later, people began to trickle back to the pepper fields when the picking season rolled around. Another factor in the increased supply of labor was the growing presence of Southeast Asian refugees in southern Louisiana. While the Vietnamese have generally chosen to earn their livings on the water by fishing and shrimping, many of the first-generation refugees from land-locked Laos gravitated into filling what little demand existed for agricultural labor.

Even though Willie Doré could count on drawing from 160 to 200 pickers out to the fields in any given day during the 1986 harvest season—three times as many as in 1978, and many of them strong men in their thirties and forties—it was clear that the days when the McIlhenny Company supplied its raw product needs with home-grown peppers were gone for good. Latin Americans performed the same day's labor for about one-tenth the wage, and even with the cost of transportation the company came out way ahead by growing in Latin America. About 98 percent of the peppers that the McIlhenny Company turned into mash in 1986 were grown and harvested in Latin America. By 1998, Willy Doré had retired and pickers were scarce once again, but it did not matter, because virtually all of the McIlhennys' peppers continued to come from south of the border.

Harvesting is only one step in the yearly cycle of the peppers. On Avery Island, all phases of this cycle were traditionally done by hand, from beginning the seeds in the greenhouse in January to turning the frozen, bare pepper bushes over into the ground the following December.

"When we plant, we got a machine that makes a little hole to put the plant in, but that's it," said Willie Doré. "Everything else by hand, don'tcha know? One person puts it in the hole and another comes along behind and covers it up.

"Then you got your weedin', and that has to be done. It's a good thing they be comin' out with chemicals we can use. If it wouldn't be for herbicides, the farmers would be in a hell of a shape, cher. It takes a long time to clear one of 'em with the government, you know? We got one clear, and one practically clear. Should be clear next year.

"This time of year we start to get that north wind and the weeds won't grow anymore, but a lot of the time I'm stuck with too many acres where you can hardly see the peppers for the weeds that grew up before that north wind came. The pickers don't want to pick where you have a lot of grass, 'cause that's where the snakes be. You be busy pickin' and you never notice the darn thing. No, *cher*, I wouldn't like to pick in grass, myself. People will pick about halfway down the bush and that's it. They not goin' no lower. That snake gonna have to jump to get their hand. Might get their leg, but not their hand."

He laughed. "You know in all my time here I never heard of nobody actually gettin' bit by a snake. We've got all kinds here, including rattlesnakes, but nobody ever been bit. So really the snakes are not that bad, but I guess none of the pickers wants to be the first."

*

The weighing was finished, and another harvest day was done. The school buses had rumbled off toward New Iberia, and the truck was bearing the boxes of peppers to the processing plant on another part of the island. Edmund, Willie, and I were joined in the suddenly quiet, empty field by Gene Jefferies, the man in charge of the company's foreign operations.

He was a tall, muscular man in his early forties, with light brown hair and pale blue eyes. He had a sincere, straightforward manner. It was easy to see how his forthrightness and confidence would be an asset in dealing with farmers in tropical countries, to say nothing of the fact that he spoke Spanish fluently.

Gene rode along with Edmund and me, and instead of retracing the route by which we had arrived, Edmund turned the car in the other direction. The road described a circle, more or less, around Avery Island, and we drove back the long way. As we came around a curve, we surprised two turkey buzzards by the side of the road, feeding on a dead armadillo. They flapped their huge wings and lifted their ponderous black bulks into the air. The armadillo had obviously been hit by a car. Armadillos are weak-sighted, slow-moving, and nearly deaf. In southern Louisiana and Texas, 'dillos dot the roadsides, second only to human beings in highway fatalities.

Edmund stopped his car by a large pond. The distant bank melted into marsh and trees. In the middle of the pond was a large cypress, its trunk ten feet around. We got out of the car and stood at the water's edge. Edmund told me there was an old bull alligator that lived in the pond and would answer to his name. He cupped his hands around his mouth and shouted, "Here, George, come here old boy. Here, George."

He seemed serious. "I don't know where he is today. Sleeping some-where. Too lazy to come out. There are alligators in all the ponds. They protect the birds from predators like raccoons."

We got back in the car. I was just as glad old George was occupied elsewhere. Only the day before I had read an article in the *Daily Iberian* with a New Orleans dateline:

> Eight-year-old Thad Little has stopped having nightmares now, and his leg is just about healed; only a few claw marks and a long surgical scar remain.
>
> Four months ago he was mauled by an old bull alligator. "He has a terrific scar but he goes to basketball practice every night. He's doing great," says Mrs. Mae Doris Little, Thad's mother.
>
> The youngster was attacked as he and some friends played in the shallows of a pond near his home in the small Cameron Parish community of Hackberry.

We swung by the processing plant and pulled up only moments after the truck had arrived, the peppers still warm from the sun. When they first reached the plant, the boxes were cleaned of any immature peppers or leafy material. Then the ripe peppers were crushed into a mash with salt, at a ratio of about eight pounds of salt for every hun-dred pounds of peppers. The mash was put immediately into barrels made exclusively from Arkansas white oak. Each barrel was sealed with a round wooden lid. There were holes drilled in the lids, so that the gases given off by the aging mash would be able to escape. Once the lid was in place, it was covered by a solid layer of salt, six inches thick. The salt allowed the gases to pass through it, while it covered the holes in the lid and kept foreign matter out of the mash. The middle-aged man who was sealing the barrels had inherited the job from his father.

The sealed barrels were stored in a warehouse. Here they would stay until they finished working. Then, after three years of aging, the mash would be mixed with vinegar, stored and stirred during a final month, and bottled as Tabasco Sauce. We followed the newly sealed barrels of mash into the warehouse and stood in the warm shadows, listening to some five hundred barrels of pepper mash in different stages of aging belch and burp gas. The smell of the mash was raw and potent, pervading the walls and clinging to clothing. Thirty seconds of standing in that warehouse was enough to clear the head and dry out the sinuses. It is, in fact, well known among bartenders that a few drops of Tabasco Sauce in a glass of soda water will dry up a cold for about an hour. Predictably, employees of the McIlhenny Company who work around the mash report they rarely suffer from colds, hay fever, or sinus trouble.

Gene Jefferies explained that in Latin America he always gave farmers strict instructions to mash and seal the peppers in the barrels within twenty-four hours after they were picked. It was also part of his job to see that the farmers had an adequate supply of Arkansas white oak barrels. He had encountered a few problems convincing farmers of the care that needed to be taken with each step of the process.

"Some of these guys have been a little lazy about going around and punching the salt out of the holes in the tops of the barrels," he said. "There have been some explosions when the lids of the barrels blew off under the accumulated pressure of the gas. Then they decided the barrels had been too full so they took to not filling them properly. We've also had an occasional problem with minor port officials in Colombia insisting on opening the barrels to check for marijuana, and not being careful about how they reseal them, so that the mash is spoiled by the time it reaches here."

Despite the small annoyances associated with doing business south of the border, Gene Jefferies stressed that he was extremely optimistic about the future of the McIlhenny Company in Latin America. We made an appointment to talk about it at a later date. He and Edmund bid me good evening at my car. They suggested I use the remaining half hour of daylight to visit the bird sanctuary. It is only at dawn and dusk that the population of Avery Island's Bird City can be appreciated. During the rest of the day, its avian residents range far and wide over the surrounding parishes in their forays for food.

At one end of the bird sanctuary is a high observation tower. I climbed it and watched the birds fly in for the night as sunset streaked the blue sky with pink and gold. I identified the white ibis, wood stork, cattle egret, snowy egret, little blue heron, and Louisiana heron. Many of the birds roosted on platforms built on high stilts in the middle of the pond. Beneath them, alligators glided soundlessly through the water, only their eyes and snouts breaking the surface.

It was autumn, and large numbers of birds had already departed for southern climes, but multitudes still filled the air. They settled in the brush and trees surrounding the pond, until every available branch seemed to hold its full quota of birds, chattering, preening, making themselves comfortable in anticipation of the coming nightfall. Purple gallinules paddled through the dense water hyacinths at the edge of the pond, honking their strange notes. The voices of the birds filled the dusk. Darkness and silence fell together.

I drove back to New Iberia and stopped at Provost's for dinner. I was barely in time to eat. Richard was closing early so he could go home and watch the World Series in the comfort of his living room, without having to get up and wait on a customer.

I went back to the Teche, turned on the television in the lobby, and settled down to cheer on the Dodgers. Al came through the front door of the hotel, just returning from his steak dinner. He flopped his big frame beside me on the couch.

"Shit almighty," he muttered. "Ah wouldn't have come back to watch TV if ah'd known it was gonna have to be baseball."

"It's the World Series," I countered.

His voice got louder. "If ah jist had a TV in mah room, ah wouldn't have to watch this baseball. Goddamn, ah cain't stand baseball."

"Put on whatever you want." Stifling my anger, I went out to walk through the warm Louisiana night. As I passed the cemetery a few blocks west of the hotel, an owl flew hooting over my head. I walked on to a large cane field at the edge of town.

The sugar cane harvest had begun, and there was a smell in the air that would remain for the entire eighty days or so that the cane was being gathered. It was an odor compounded of burning fields and smoke from the mills, a smell that was the essence of molasses. It was a piercing, sickly sweetness, something like the way a drop of milk smells as it curdles on your skin.

It takes a stalk of cane three years to reach maturity. When a field of Louisiana cane was ready to be harvested, it was set afire. The flames did not consume the cane, but they did burn off the leafy shucks. The stalks smoldered, weakened, and eventually toppled to the ground. A large machine with huge steel pincers was driven through the rows. Its arthropoid claw clamped the cane, lifted it high off the ground, swiveled on a turret, and dropped it into a truck that moved through the field beside it. Sometimes big wagons pulled by tractors were used instead of trucks to transport the cane from field to mill.

The stalks were packed into truck or wagon until there did not seem to be room for one more stalk without losing the whole top-heavy load. During harvest season, the pavement around railroad tracks and bumps in the road was covered with pulverized cane that had been jarred off and crushed beneath traffic. When it reached the mill, the cane was crushed, boiled, and spun. One acre of land produced an average of twenty-five tons. One ton of cane yielded 180 pounds of raw sugar at the mill. Day and night, the fields burned, the trucks and wagons lumbered through town, and the vast mills poured out white smoke from their stacks.

My anger at being driven out of Yankee Stadium and the Teche Hotel lobby had faded. I stood and watched flames flicker and dance through the cane field. The harvest moon rose full and orange behind the thick smoke from the smoldering cane. I leaned against a tall pecan tree at the edge of the field. Somewhere high up in its branches, a mockingbird trilled a frenzied nighttime medley.

rs. Dorothy Spencer was a stout black lady in her early forties. She and her family lived in a small wooden house on West Pershing Street, one of those streets paved with clamshells in downtown New Iberia, just south of the railroad tracks. The windows of their four-room clapboard house were filmed with the white dust raised by passing cars. Inside, the house was shadowy and cool.

Her eldest daughter, Karen, was in her first year at the University of Southwestern Louisiana in Lafayette, twenty miles away. "Yes indeed, that chile gone ter get her education. Not like me. When I was her age I was goin' out to Avery Island, workin' in the fields, pickin' those peppers.

"They used to carry us out there on a truck. It would still be dark. It was the barest light, just enough to try and get out there and pick. I'd tie a can in my front, and a can in my back. We'd dump the cans in our box when they got full and that way you didn't have to be takin' that box through them rows, 'cause that would sure be hard on you.

"Those fields are beautiful to see first thing in the mornin'. It be foggy when you get out there. Sometime you get a nice breeze. Then you don't mind pickin'. It don't be too warm. The best time of year to pick 'em is when the weather just gettin' cool. Sometime, later on in the year, they make a fire on the headland and you can warm up, go back, warm up, go back. Tha's nice."

Everyone in southern Louisiana, from Dorothy Spencer to Walter

McIlhenny, uses the word dinner to refer to the midday repast, and supper to designate the evening meal. "By the time dinner rolls around that sun is out and it's hot in those fields. Maybe you're pickin' where there's some trees and you can go over under 'em and eat your dinner, or maybe there ain't no trees and you eat in the sun. I'd usually make half a box of peppers before dinner and half a box afterwards.

"Soon as I got my box filled up someone was sure to say, 'Fill another one, you'll make more money.' But I wouldn't do it. I wasn't greedy. And by that time my hand was burnin', *cher*. Sometimes I'd catch one of those peppers and break it in my hand by accident. Oh child! One time I got some in my mouth and eyes and I swore I wasn't goin' back, but I went back a few more times.

"Yes, *cher*, it be beautiful out there in the mornin', but those peppers really do burn to pick. It's bad in the mornin' when the dew's out, but it's worse when the sun comes out. Those rows are long. You got to bend for those peppers. You got to go low. They say you supposed to pick 'em with two hands, but I never learned how to do it. I'd always keep one hand on my hip when I bent down. Maybe that's why I had so many breakin' in my hand.

"There's a lot of things to scare you up in that field. Like rattlesnakes. If you're pickin' under a bush and you hear those rattles, it's gone ter scare you. It happened to me. I was goin' for a bush and I seen that snake. I hollered. Me, I hollered. And they got a man over from the headland. See, maybe that snake strayed away from the Jungle Gardens and they don't like to kill 'em, but sometimes, *cher*, they got to."

We were sitting in the dim light of her living room. Dorothy Spencer was in an old wooden rocker, hands resting in her broad lap. She rocked back and forth, laughing and enjoying her memories. She chuckled and said, "At the end of the day along comes the truck to weigh your peppers. My first day I made four dollars. How I suffered! My little girl Karen was just a baby, then. That night I couldn't hold her, my hands hurt so much. I couldn't make her understand.

"My brother-in-law! Man, he could beat anybody pickin' peppers. You may think I'm lyin', but he could pick six to seven boxes in a day. When he left the pepper field, it would be with fifty dollars. That's what he was used to takin' home. He did it for many years. He was a pepper picker, that man. But he got cancer of the jaw and they took half of it off. That was sho' a man for peppers. It never bothered his hands. He enjoyed that work. He looked forward to pepper season.

"It just wasn't the job for me. I cook my dinner, clean my house, tend to my children in school, and I don't need the trouble of pickin' them peppers. These days children don't want to pick them. When I was my children's age I enjoyed a challenge like that, but they think they're too good for that kind of work. I had my fun when I was young. I did it. What better way to learn than to go into the fields? Now I'm forty-five years old, and I don't believe I could stoop like that." She laughed and rocked.

*

In 1968, when the McIlhennys realized the number of people willing to pick peppers was rapidly shrinking, they bought some acreage on Jefferson Island, another huge salt dome a few miles west across the marsh from Avery Island. They planted a large crop of *Capsicum frutescens* on their new property, and started trying to use a mechanical harvester to pick it.

Gene Jefferies drove me over to Jefferson Island one afternoon in a company pickup truck to see the latest experimental model. On the way he talked about the different kinds of work he had done in South America. He had first gone to Brazil with the Peace Corps. After his two-year stint, he was hired by the International Research Institute, which was funded by the Rockefellers, to stay in Brazil as a ranch management specialist. Later, they moved him to Venezuela to work in beef production. He was in Venezuela for seven years.

"My wife and I had been overseas damned near twelve years. Our kids were scattered all over in schools, and my wife was anxious to come back to the States. We did, and I ended up with the McIlhenny Company. I love my job."

Half of Jefferies's time was spent traveling in Central and South America. The other half was based in his office on Avery Island. When he was home, one of his jobs was to oversee the experiments with the mechanical harvester.

"The Mark Two looks pretty good," he told me on the way to Jefferson Island, "but there's still a heck of a lot of room for improvement. It's doing pretty well today. I went over this morning and increased the water pressure, which seemed to help. I timed the operation, and they can come to the end of a row, take off the boxes, fill the machine back up with water, put the empty boxes on, and be ready to go down the next row in four minutes. Of course, I was standing there timing them," he laughed.

We arrived at the Jefferson Island pepper fields. The pepper bushes were thriving, each one covered with ripe fruit. The Jefferson Island fields were flatter than those at Avery Island and had better drainage. The soil was good and the peppers did well there. The problem was getting them off the bush.

We watched the Mark Two go down a row of bushes. It was driven by a middle-aged man in a tan company uniform. It was a mammoth machine, made up of a large metal shroud attached to the bottom of a high tractor. The driver wore earplugs; the Mark Two's roar was deafening. As it lurched down the row, the ground shook and dust rose in thick clouds. The picking mechanism was a simple idea: the shroud covered the pepper bushes and sprayed them with jets of water. The ripe peppers were knocked loose and fell onto a conveyor belt, which carried them back to a box mounted at the rear of the tractor. The belt dumped the peppers into the box as it turned to go back under for another pass.

After the Mark Two had passed down the row, there were a sizable number of red peppers still standing, glistening and wet on the dripping bush. "That's part of the problem," Jefferies admitted. "We can vary the water pressure from zero to six hundred pounds. If you crank it up to six hundred you just strip the bush. To find where it is that you get the reds and leave the greens is harder than you might think. A lot harder."

Nobody at the McIlhenny Company was satisfied with the Mark Two, but everyone agreed it was an improvement over the Mark One, Schellstede and Associates' first attempt to build a harvester. The Mark One was housed, in what appeared to be permanent retirement, in a barn on Jefferson Island. It was a massive piece of machinery, the size of a grain combine, whereas the Mark Two had been designed so that the picking shroud easily detached and left a perfectly normal tractor behind.

The two harvesters were not cheap to build. The Mark Two cost about $50,000, half for the tractor and half for the picking shroud and machinery. Late in 1978, Schellstede and Associates submitted a prospectus for a Mark Three to Ned Simmons and Walter McIlhenny. The Mark Three was projected as a three-row machine, a monster tractor over a giant picking shroud. It was hypothesized that what would be lost in maneuverability would be offset by harvesting three rows simultaneously.

The McIlhenny Company decided not to invest in the Mark Three, and they have not regretted that decision. By 1982, they had stopped experimenting on Jefferson Island. Gene Jefferies and the small farmers he contracts with in Latin America proved themselves capable of providing whatever level of production was needed. Gene was not surprised. Even when I spoke with him initially, in 1978, he had been convinced that the McIlhenny Company's future lay in Central and South America.

"I feel that most of the Latin countries produce a pepper that is even better than those from Avery Island," he told me. "Down there, for instance, they can afford to sort every box of peppers. I think the minimum wage in Honduras is three dollars a day, and in Nicaragua it's down around two dollars.

"In Honduras, they'll pick the peppers, bring them to a shed, and women stand around and pick out anything that's not perfect. So, if we're careful and set up good mills for them, along with a lot of supervision on the mashing and storing in the barrels, we end up with just as good a mash as we produce here. I was down in Guatemala this year when they were harvesting, and those plants were loaded with a fine crop."

Avery Island is closer to Guatemala than to New York, and it used to take Gene Jefferies only a few hours to fly there from New Orleans. "In Guatemala, we have a farmer on Lake Isabel. You fly out to a landing strip and he picks you up in a boat. You go across the river, get into a bigger boat and drive thirty minutes up the lake. Then you pull into a tiny village, leave the boat, and walk about a mile and a half back through the jungle. You get there and realize he has just cut this big field out of the jungle.

"They can keep tabascos growing all year down there, as long as they rotate their fields. The man we contract with uses practically all Indian labor. He has to find a straw boss who's bilingual, who speaks Spanish and the Indian dialect. They fertilize plant by plant. One guy comes along with a sharp stick and makes a little hole. Then another guy comes along behind and drops in a little fertilizer.

"They throw structures up out there to house the grinding operation and store the barrels of mash. Then they'll load the barrels on a wagon, haul them back through the jungle, and bring them down the river. It doesn't take so long for the mash to stop working down there, because of the hotter temperatures, and when it's done that's when he'll send it up here to us. It's not easy for him to get those Arkansas white oak barrels in and out of there. He can only get about ten at a time on his boat. But he can still get the whole thing done cheaper there than we could do it here."

That was in 1978. By 1980, however, the political situation in Guatemala had become extremely unstable. The McIlhenny Company decided to abandon their efforts there and concentrate on Honduras, Colombia, Venezuela, and, to a lesser degree, Mexico.

"Until the devaluation of its currency, Venezuela was a very high-cost country, and for our major contractor it just wasn't worth it to grow peppers at the price we were paying," Gene Jefferies told me in the summer of 1986.

"We jacked the price up, and shortly after that they had a devaluation, so it made it very favorable for him and he's gone from two hundred barrels three years ago to over fifteen hundred in 1985. The economics there have changed considerably, so we have three real good countries now: Venezuela, Colombia, and Honduras."

There were, however, some problems associated with growing peppers in Latin America. One of them was disease. Hot peppers were susceptible to over a score of viruses, many of which could wipe out a field. Even in southern Louisiana, viruses were generally expected to claim about 20 percent of any given year's crop. Among the most common and deadly of them were tobacco etch, tomato spotted wilt, and bacterial wilt.

Cajuns have known for many years that if tabasco peppers and tobacco are grown close together, the peppers will die. Despite the fact
that tobacco and pepper are both members of the solanacaeous family,
they cannot coexist. Even the smoking of tobacco has traditionally
been prohibited in the pepper fields. It is now known that the virus is
spread from the tobacco by aphids. Tobacco etch only slightly affects
the growth of tobacco, but it can devastate a crop of *Capsicum frutescens*.

In Honduras, tobacco had been grown for centuries in some of the
same regions where Gene Jefferies found farmers who were willing
and able to grow tabascos. The Honduran government offered its co-
operation to the company. An agreement was reached that specified
the company would financially support pepper research in Honduras,
and the government would see to it that tobacco was not grown in certain areas.

Hot peppers are vulnerable to other calamities besides viruses. An
insect called the pepper weevil is widespread in Mexico and Central
America. At least twice, the McIlhenny Company lost an entire season's crop in Mexico to weevils. They are relentless predators. The
female makes a tiny hole in the pepper and deposits an egg inside.
The worm pupates, and when it is mature, it drills a hole in the wall
of the pepper and comes out.

Until 1975, the pepper weevil had never been seen in southern
Louisiana. That year it appeared in plague proportions, wiping out 80
percent of the crop on Avery Island and in surrounding parishes. It
was believed that the weevils had arrived with a shipment of hot peppers destined for one of New Iberia's hot sauce manufacturers.

Farmers in the tropics use an insecticide, Sevin, against the weevils,
but it was not until 1977 that North American farmers received permission from the United States Department of Agriculture (USDA) to use
it. When the female weevil stings a tabasco pepper and deposits her
egg, the pepper falls from the bush. This is fortunate, because as soon
as a pepper grower sees the first peppers start to fall, the field can be
sprayed and the remainder of the crop may be saved. The McIlhennys
used a product called Sevimol, which was a mixture of molasses and
Sevin that stuck to a bush. Spraying was accomplished on Avery Island
with relative ease, but according to Gene Jefferies it did not prove so
simple in Mexico or Central America. Unless the Latin farmers were

closely supervised, or were unusually reliable about following instructions, there was a possibility they would use too much or too little on their fields.

If a farmer must err, it is always preferable to do so on the side of too little, though it may mean the loss of a crop. Unfortunately, most Latin American countries do not enforce strict controls on the use of pesticides and herbicides. The farmers in these countries often live in remote areas and have never heard of, or not paid much attention to, the dangers attached to the excessive use of chemicals. Companies whose products have been banned for health reasons in the United States are not above using such countries for dumping grounds. It was part of Gene Jefferies's job to explain USDA regulations to the farmers, and to impress them with the need to follow his instructions about which chemicals, and what quantities of them, should be used.

Since Gene Jefferies could not personally supervise each farmer during the entire growing season, the McIlhenny Company spot-checked each shipment of mash that arrived at Avery Island from a foreign country. In this fashion, they hoped to detect any mash made from peppers exposed to one or more chemicals prohibited by the USDA. A private laboratory near New Iberia took samples from a few barrels in each shipment and tested them for a selected list of chemicals which should not be there. Testing each sample cost around two hundred dollars in 1986.

Politics was the other major stumbling block to growing peppers in Latin America. For instance, in 1977 a Honduran who grew for the company on some of his land ran into an old schoolmate from Nicaragua named Sanchez, who was a general in Anastasio Somoza's army and the director of the Telecommunications Ministry. The Honduran told General Sanchez about his arrangements with the McIlhenny Company. Sanchez had several farms and two sons. The younger son was underemployed and played around at managing the farms. Sanchez called the McIlhenny Company in December 1977, and spoke with Gene Jefferies.

"General Sanchez said that he would be interested in growing some peppers for us. Normally, we would just say all right and put his name in a file, but Walter McIlhenny being a general, and this guy being a general, Walter said to send him a couple of ounces of seed and see what happened. I sent him the seeds and some instructions. We never heard anything more. In July, I got a call from his second son, Ricardo Sanchez, saying he's got six thousand plants loaded with fruit, and what should he do with them?

"I was on my way to Central America, anyhow, so I went by and saw him. We started figuring how I could get some of the barrels into the country. Then, the revolution against Somoza broke out and I haven't been back since. We did prove they could grow pepper there."

The company simply wrote the Nicaraguan experience off as a loss. In the years since the Sandanistas came to power, there have been some inquiries from individual farmers about growing peppers, but these have not been pursued. Since the company had not been counting on the peppers that Ricardo Sanchez was growing, the loss was not serious. But the loss of a year's crop in Honduras or Venezuela or Colombia could result in a shortage of mash from which to make Tabasco Sauce. While the company does not run the risk of nationalization, since it merely enters into contractual agreements with local landowners and does not own the land, it does have to worry about political instability, which could suddenly render a year's crop inaccessible.

Despite volatile politics, and an increased risk of crop disease, growing peppers south of the border has proved as successful as the mechanical harvesters were unsuccessful. Production figures held up in Latin America, during the first decade of the company's investments there, and even bordered, at times, on being too much of a good thing. In 1978, the company filled 5,200 barrels with mash, and in 1980 that figure jumped to 13,200.

"That was kind of a freak year," said Gene Jefferies. "We were going crazy trying to get barrels down there. Every year we plant about the same acreage, but it seems like every year you get some dry weather in Honduras or some disease problem in Colombia, or something that tends to balance out, but that particular year everything seemed to work well.

"So that really added to our inventory. In '81 we started feeling comfortable about beginning to control some of our planting acreage and we produced right at 9,400 barrels. In '82 it was 8,200. In '83 we jumped back up a little bit. We were back up to about 12,000 barrels.

It was another of those years where everything fell into place. I started getting a little worried about producing too much. '84 and '85 were both a little over 10,000 barrels. Unless I see a real big change in our sales this year, I think we'll have to start seriously cutting back on production in '87."

Sales did climb, partly because of the amplification of the number of ways in which Tabasco Sauce was marketed. By 1998, peppers for about 15,000 barrels worth of mash were being grown in Central and South America, and McIlhenny imported virtually all of its tabasco peppers, primarily from Colombia, Honduras, Brazil, and Costa Rica. Central and South America accounted for virtually all the company's tabasco peppers. In some countries, one agent represented a group of small farmers in dealing with the company, while in others, Gene Jefferies continued to buy directly from multiple farmers, each with a small plot.

The transportation system has been refined, and since 1990, instead of shipping barrels, the company now takes the mash in barrels to the nearest port and pumps it into a stainless steel container, which comes by ship to New Orleans and then on the back of a flat-bed truck to Avery Island, where it is pumped into barrels. The containers have paddles inside which stir the mash at regular intervals during the journey. This has eliminated the problem of barrels being sealed incorrectly by Latin farmers, but on the days when the containers arrive, the plant has to be ready for them, and everything demands precise organization.

Gene Jefferies was sixty-two years old in 1999, nearing retirement age, and the company realized that having become entirely dependent on importing tabasco peppers, it would have to hire someone who could learn from him — someone who spoke Spanish, understood agriculture, and could oversee the large operation from the remote growing fields to the arrival of the stainless steel containers full of crushed peppers.

Their search for Jefferies's successor turned up Greg Tate, who was born in Brooklyn, has a masters in agriculture sciences from Cornell University, spent time working in Venezuela with the Peace Corps, and was hired in 1994 as Gene Jefferies's second in command. He has a square, engaging face, wears steel-rimmed spectacles and is black, the first African American to reach the executive ranks of the McIlhenny Company and have his own office on the second floor of the Avery Island headquarters. Gene Jefferies had nothing but praise for his work.

*

It was late in the afternoon when I returned to the Teche Hotel from Jefferson Island. My landlady, Miz Marie, looked out her apartment door as I passed through the lobby. She called to me, "M'sieu. M'sieu. Please come in and meet my husband. He is down these last few years with a lung sickness. I told him about you and he is eager to make your acquaintance. It would mean very much to him."

I went inside their apartment. Her fifty-year-old husband was sitting tall and emaciated in a reclining chair watching television. He wore a bathrobe and pajamas. A set of remote controls was in his hand. As I entered, he clicked the volume down below the audible level, but left the picture on. It was the evening news, a riot in some foreign city, Beirut by the look of it. Beside the chair stood a tall tank of oxygen. He spoke with the gasping-for-air intonation typical of deteriorating lungs.

"This was Marie's hotel. She's the Cajun. When I met her she was running it alone. I was a construction worker. Originally from Tennessee. It's a good hotel. Clean, reasonable. . . ." He had a coughing spasm and reached into the folds of his robe to extract a handkerchief. He spit into it.

"Just two types of people I don't allow here: niggers and women. White people wouldn't stay here if I rented to colored. Women are always hanging their stockings and underwear around to dry. Leaves water on the floor. Men are much neater than women. Say, I'm really glad to meet a writer."

According to an article in the *American Journal of Epidemiology*, a white male had a better chance of getting lung cancer in southern Louisiana than practically anywhere else in the world. Between 1950 and 1969, twenty-seven parishes in southern Louisiana were among the hundred counties in the United States with the highest death rate for white males from the disease. Acadiana's civic boosters attributed these statistics to the devil-may-care attitude of Cajuns toward cigarette smoking, but many others believed it was the pollutants produced by the petroleum industry since 1949 that were responsible. This latter interpretation was supported by studies which found that white men who lived in areas where the economy is tied to the paper, petroleum, or chemical industries had a significantly higher chance of dying of lung cancer. I could not help but wonder what the real price was that the residents of Acadiana had paid in exchange for giving up their self-sufficiency and joining the consumer economy of late twentieth-century North America.

arville, Louisiana, site of the only hospital in the United States for victims of leprosy, is seventy miles northeast of New Iberia and thirty miles southeast of Baton Rouge. I finished a day's research at the Louisiana State University library in Baton Rouge and, on an impulse, turned off Interstate 10 for a quick drive down to Carville. What appeared on the map to be a forty-minute drive took me two hours.

A narrow road led through the tiny town of Grosse Tete (Big Head) and wound southward along Bayou Boeuf (Bayou Beef). At one point I saw three deer—buck, doe, and fawn—grazing by the roadside. They raised their heads and stood quivering and alert, but they did not bound away as the car passed. A little further on, a young black woman appeared by the edge of the road. She was barefoot, lithe and graceful, with a bundle wrapped in a white sheet balanced on her head, steadied by one upraised hand. I watched in the rearview mirror as she crossed the road. A quick, fluid step carried her out of sight among the trees.

The road came out of the woods, into Plaquemine (pronounced plack-a-min), seat of Iberville Parish. The town was built on the Mississippi River, and cars, trailer trucks, and heavy equipment jammed its streets. Dust and exhaust fumes hung in the air, traffic crept along, horns honked, brakes squealed, and jackhammers pounded. I drove through town to a ferry crossing and joined a line of cars under the blazing sun to wait for the free ferry. It was one of many which the state operated at different points along the river.

The other side of the river was open country with an occasional cleared field or tumbledown house. I followed the road for another ten miles before reaching Carville. Talk about a small town. There was one general store and a few houses. The road ran on alongside the high bank of a levee which blocked the river from view. A few miles past the general store I came upon the incongruously manicured lawns and baroque buildings of the United States Health Service Public Hospital.

The isolation of this spot and its proximity to the river were the two main reasons why it was chosen by the state, in 1894, as the site for a leprosarium. Residents of the area were informed that the new buildings outside Carville were for an ostrich farm. The lepers were brought upriver from New Orleans under cover of darkness. Five years passed before the state allowed word of what was going on at the hospital to circulate through nearby communities.

Leprosy was, and still is, one of the most widely misunderstood of diseases. Only prolonged intimate exposure can result in transmission between people, yet the very word "leprosy" inspires such terror that there has been a long campaign by its victims to change the name of the disease. They prefer to call it Hansen's Disease—after G. A. Hansen, a Norwegian, who first saw the M. leprae bacillus under a microscope—in hopes of reducing the burden of hysteria and ignorance which patients have historically endured.

The hospital was actually more sanatorium than hospital. It was built in the style of institutional architecture that was prevalent at the turn of the century among Public Health Service hospitals. It had acres of green lawns and massive old white buildings, with long stretches of elevated, window-lined walkways. The hospital was staffed by nuns from the Daughters of Charity of Saint Vincent de Paul. As I strolled the neat gravel paths around the grounds, I encountered the sisters, baskets hanging from their arms, placidly gathering nuts in the shade of huge pecan trees.

Hansen's Disease involves a degeneration of the nerves, beginning with a loss of feeling at the extremities of the body which moves inward. The first treatment for the disease was developed by researchers at Carville during the 1940s. Sulfone drugs were found to be effective in holding Hansen's Disease in check, but if a patient stopped taking the drugs, the disease returned in full force. People with Hansen's Disease who came to Carville were expected to remain there for the rest of their lives. The population was fixed at around three hundred, and there was a long waiting list, made up of people from all over the world.

Patients who wanted to take jobs or classes were encouraged to do so. There was a daily commuter service from the hospital to Baton Rouge. A full social life was also available, and there had been marriages. A pond on the hospital grounds was stocked annually with bass and bluegill. There was a restaurant. Food, cigarettes, and toiletries were available at wholesale prices from the grocery. There were two bars. There was also a full printing press in one building, where patients published and printed a bi-monthly magazine called The Star, which had a circulation of 75,000.

Night had fallen by the time I left the hospital grounds. An ivory crescent moon was already sinking behind the levee. I followed the road to White Castle and caught a ferry across the dark waters of the Mississippi. Rather than retrace my steps through Plaquemine, I turned south and drove through Pierre Part toward Morgan City.

The road ran beside a bayou—as do many roads in this part of the country—but it was too dark to distinguish between land and water. Suddenly a broad shaft of light appeared in the deep night on the banks of the bayou. It was a large bulb mounted on a pole, and it illuminated the end of a dock and a circle of water beyond it. On the end of the wharf were sitting three generations of men: one young, one middle-aged, and one old. Each held a cane pole extended over the water. The scene flashed by my car window and was gone.

I reached Morgan City and stopped at an open cafe for a bowl of gumbo and a Jax Beer before heading on to New Iberia. While I ate, I listened to the only other customer in the place talk to the waitress. He was about sixty, big and fat, but still with an air of great strength in his massive frame. He was speaking about how his parents had been divorced when he was fifteen.

"Some days I would just sneak away from school and come on home. I just wanted to hide all the time, you know? Lord, I suffered so much for the shame of that divorce. Kids today don't have any idea of what it was like then. A divorce is nothing today. Oh Lord, how that hurt me!"

The waitress, also middle-aged, was lean and intense. Her black hair was up in a bouffant. She nodded vigorously and replied, "Kids today don't know a thing. Ever watch 'em dance? You call that disco stuff dancing? Not me, *cher.* I don't call that dancing, me. They're killing our jitterbug. Killing it! These kids don't know about anything."

The man finished his beer and left. The waitress made me for a receptive ear, and sat down at my table as I spooned up the last of the tasty gumbo. She was nursing a grudge against City Hall and, having no other way to protest, was anxious to spread the word. The Saint Mary's Parish Police Jury (the equivalent in Louisiana of a county commission) had recently passed an ordinance requiring all people who applied for work in the parish to obtain a special identification card at the courthouse. Her son, who was seventeen, had gotten a job at a local shipyard and was required to have a card.

"That's no damned foreigner, that's my son," she said, outraged. "My son, born and raised right here. Just like me. You should see the questions they made him answer for that card. It's a long form. I said, 'Soon they'll be telling me I can't work if I don't answer a bunch of questions that are none of their business.' Then they took my son's fingerprints. I said, 'I'll be damned. So it's come to that now. . . .' "

It came to that because a surprising number of known and, frequently, wanted criminals began turning up in Morgan City during petroleum's boom years. It had become an underground railroad station on a dubious circuit, and was beginning to rival Alaska as a place where good money could be made in a law-abiding fashion without jeopardizing one's anonymity. There was plenty of roustabout work there, and if the job got done nobody was going to ask for details about a man's past. There are places for laundering men, as well as money, and Morgan City became a favorite among both organized criminals and freelancers. In 1981, for instance, when writer Norman Mailer's con-wise protégé Jack Henry Abbott killed a young man in New York and fled, he went to Morgan City, where he was found months later with a job and a rented room.

The identification card scheme did not work, of course. Shortly after being put into effect it was declared unconstitutional in the

Louisiana courts. But by that time the price of oil was falling, and the problem of what to do with all the transients who came through looking for work no longer existed.

During the oil boom, there were more problems resulting from southern Louisiana's rapidly swelling population than whether it would become necessary for everyone to carry an identification card. It proved difficult for the region to absorb all the skilled workers and professionals who had moved their families from the North, East, or West to Acadiana. Many of them were pipefitters, electricians, or mechanics. Others were among the shoals of engineers and attorneys who swam around the petroleum industry. All of those people brought some well-defined expectations. One was that they would find decent and available housing. In a town like New Iberia, where there had not been much excess housing before the boom, the real estate market was tight as a tick. By 1978, things had reached crisis proportions.

When Miz Marie told me that I was getting a bargain at the Teche Hotel for twenty-five dollars a week, she meant square business. Anywhere else in town that room would have cost me seventy-five. And things got worse if more than one room was required. Trailer courts were completely filled. Every apartment in town had a long waiting list. Housing developments, of which there were only a handful, were sold before the ground was broken. Local builders did not want to bother putting up tract houses. They preferred to construct homes in the eighty-, ninety-, and hundred-thousand-dollar market, which they could sell as fast as they could finish them. Other big money-makers were fast food restaurants, convenience stores, and shopping malls. Between 1975 and 1978, three shopping centers were built in New Iberia, and each housed a number of national outlets. There was plenty of disposable income in Iberia Parish. All of the construction activity provided jobs and created incentives for more people to come to New Iberia. So it went. Boom town economics.

But it was over almost before it began. By 1986, there were plenty of available rooms, apartments, trailers, condos, and estates. Lots of space was available in the shopping centers, with empty stores standing in the malls like numerous gaps in what used to be a mouthful of teeth. The only consumer item in short supply, Cajuns joked ruefully, was U-Haul trailers. Unemployment was at 20 percent and lots of people had left. Those who were important enough to their corporations had been transferred to Alaska, or the North Sea, or Saudi Arabia, and those whose jobs were expendable had been let go, and had left southern Louisiana to look for work elsewhere. Houses sold for half of what people had paid for them a few years before, if they could be sold at all. The people who stayed in Acadiana after the boom passed were mostly those who had been there before the boom arrived, many of them left with only a heavy burden of debt by which to remember those few years when it had seemed like there would always be money to spend.

Many a grand project came to naught. There were, for instance, big plans for the expansion of the Acadiana Regional Airport, just west of New Iberia. It was nothing more than a few runways and hangars in the middle of a large field which had been built as a naval base in the mid-1960s, then abandoned four years later by the Navy and sold to Iberia Parish at a rock-bottom price. But developers foresaw a multi-million dollar international trade center, an industrial park, and a transportation center for the petroleum industry. That there was a perfectly good airport only twenty miles away in Lafayette did not dim local enthusiasm for the airport project.

Gaston Mestayer (pronounced *met-a-yea*) was the secretary of the Chamber of Commerce when I met him in 1978. "I was tickled to death to get that airport," he told me. "We worked for a long time to get the police jury to proceed in such a manner that it could be an airport, plus an industrial park, and everything else. The development of the airport has mostly been a Chamber of Commerce project. Right now, we've got three-quarters occupancy leased out there. We'll start to build soon. There's no doubt in my mind that eventually the airport in Lafayette will move over here. Take-offs and landings will increase every day. . . ."

The fact that it did not work out like that was not Gaston Mestayer's fault. He was an enthusiastic, friendly man of nearly sixty years, balding, relaxed, his skin uncolored by the sun. He was a tireless worker for the city of New Iberia and rarely took time to enjoy the outdoors. On holidays and Sundays he could usually be found in his office at the Chamber.

The Mestayer family had been in Louisiana nearly three hundred years. They settled first in the northern part of the state, but as early as 1736 Gaston's great-great-great-great-grandfather had moved to bayou country. According to Gaston Mestayer, this ancestor raised some cayenne peppers.

"He raised them not to eat, but to use as a medicine for asthma. My great-uncle told me how my ancestor had trouble with the Indians coming around and trying to steal the peppers because they were such strong medicine. You'll notice, for instance, how people who work out at the Tabasco factory don't suffer from asthma.

"Peppers are a real part of the memories of my childhood. I remember seeing strings of hot peppers hanging on the fences, drying in the sun. I can remember my own mother stringing them together and hanging them all around the porch. My sister could never get enough. She used to steal the Tabasco bottle and fill up a big tablespoon full and just sip away on it. My mama had to hide the bottle. We used to drive the country roads and see acres of peppers being grown for Trappey's.

"I won't eat food that's not seasoned with peppers. If I had to go on a bland diet, I don't know what I'd do. I have my own special ways of fixing my gumbos and sauces. Everybody here is like that. They all love to cook."

In 1964, New Iberians elected a man named Alan Daigre as their new mayor. He named his closest friend, Gaston Mestayer, as his executive assistant. The two men were still in office in 1978. The most serious problem that had been facing the city back in 1964, according to Gaston Mestayer, was a debt of $350,000 accumulated by previous administrations. The mayor and his executive assistant pressed the police jury to pass a 1 percent sales tax. It was duly instituted, and within two years New Iberia was in the black. In 1971, the sales tax was bringing in $69,000 a month. By 1978, that figure had skyrocketed to almost $250,000 a month. When Gaston Mestayer talked about New Iberia, he was a man talking about his favorite child, and he was reluctant to speak of its problems.

"Housing is our biggest problem. Right now, the situation is critical, and it's probably going to get worse before it gets better. There are usually fifty to sixty people a day who come into the Chamber looking for a house.

"Me, I'll say this: I'd rather have too little housing and plenty of jobs than too few jobs and plenty of housing. And, we've got the jobs. Right now there are seven hundred open jobs in Iberia Parish. Ten years ago, only three out of every fifteen people who went to college came back to New Iberia when they graduated. That has all changed. We have something for them to come back to. This parish has the lowest unemployment rate in the state of Louisiana."

By 1986, there were, indeed, too few jobs and plenty of housing, and the parish's unemployment rate was one of the highest in the nation. Gaston Mestayer was retired, but Alan Daigre was still mayor. He was facing a deficit budget for the first year since he had been in office. That debt he had worked so hard to erase had come back to haunt him. At a time when many New Iberians were having a hard time keeping their heads above water, he was faced with the need to ask for another quarter-cent hike in the sales tax—the first since 1964.

By 1998, New Iberia was in better shape. Two mayors had served since Alan Daigre finally retired from office. The second was a forward-looking woman named Ruth Fontenot, under whose administration the city had become a more liveable and attractive place according to many residents. There were no more downtown streets paved with clamshells. The stores along Main Street were freshly painted and pretty much fully occupied. A vacant building that had once housed a public high school was transformed into housing for senior citizens. There was a public parking lot in the middle of town, and the walkway along the Bayou Teche had been widened and prettied up. Richard Provost had retired, and the long building with its lovely wooden interior that had housed his bar and grill became Armand's, an upscale *nouvelle cuisine* place, where a person ate well but could expect to spend more than twenty dollars for the pleasure. The jukebox had disappeared.

When I asked Gaston Mestayer about the disproportionate rate of lung cancer among white men in Acadiana, he lit a low-tar cigarette and told me, "I believe it's strictly from smoking. People here like to enjoy themselves, even if they die young. We're heavy smokers. There's an area of New Jersey that has a higher rate of cancer than we do. Also people who work in the coal mines in Kentucky. I'm not sure our cancer rate is really higher than the rest of the country.

"We're not scared of anything having to do with oil. We've been living with it all our lives. It's our mainstay. Sixty percent of the jobs in this parish are related to the oil industry. We couldn't get along without it. People say there's a limit, but I don't see any end. Oil is always going to be needed. The oil industry is not going to ruin life down here. Just the opposite. It'll leave the good things, and make the others better. Basically, we're still going to be the same people we always were."

This sentiment was a common one back in 1978. Elected officials in Acadiana were quick to express the certainty that the coexistence of Cajun and corporate lifestyles was possible. They expounded the theory of the six-month Cajun: someone who was drinking dark-roast coffee, putting cane syrup on pancakes, cooking gumbos, and going out on Saturday night to drink and dance within six months of arrival. They insisted that Cajun culture could remain intact and still absorb legions of Americans.

What these officials did not realize, or refused to consider, was that petroleum was something essentially different from the other marketable goods in Acadiana's inventory. In the case of cotton, shrimp, fur, cane, or hot peppers, profits were concentrated in the hands of people from the parish. Even the cane industry, which generated almost $50 million in Iberia Parish in 1978, was owned almost exclusively by local interests. At the farthest remove, a few of the cane mills were owned by absentee investors in other states.

Those who controlled southern Louisiana's petroleum were as far removed as a Muslim consortium in Saudi Arabia or a multinational corporation in New York, Zurich, or London. Most of the huge profits that flowed from the oil patch were reinvested in other states and countries. This was the first time that those who were making big money from Acadiana were entirely uninvolved with the area's special qualities. The oil industry was in southern Louisiana to take the most it could get, with the least expense, for as long as it lasted. When that was done, the region and its economy would simply be abandoned, and if the resource and the market should combine to make it profitable to start up again, then another boom would be created. Until then, the industry would take its largesse elsewhere.

The phone rang. Gaston Mestayer had a long conversation with someone on the other end concerning the rates for renting a private plane. He hung up and smiled at me. "That was a gentleman calling from New Orleans. I've got to arrange for the rental of a plane next month. The Chamber of Commerce is presenting their 1978 Civil Service Award to Ronald Reagan, the ex-governor of California. We've got to rent a plane to bring him out from New Orleans. He is a very popular man here. Among the people I know, he's a hands-down favorite to be the next president."

ales of ghosts, witches, and spirits were no longer prevalent in Iberia Parish. Twentieth-century living had reduced the credibility of otherworldly manifestations, but in the old days it was commonly believed that witches went out at night and rode people, actually putting bridles on them and bits in their mouths. People who awoke in the morning with a cold sore at the corner of their lips knew they had been ridden during the night. Others were said to have awakened with dirt under their fingernails or between their toes. It was held that a person who cried out in sleep was being chased by a witch. Nightmare: to be ridden through the night.

There was a story about a witch and some red pepper which could be heard early in this century over the length and breadth of the southern states, as well as in the West Indies, the Bahamas, and the Georgia Sea Islands. It concerned a witch who took off her skin and hung it on the wall before going out to find somebody to ride. While she was gone, a man snuck in and sprinkled red pepper in the skin. When the witch returned from the ride and tried to put her skin back on, she cried, "Skinny, don't you know me? What's the matter skin? Don't you know me, my old skin?" She was discovered by the townspeople while she was hopping up and down, and was put to death.

Although people in New Iberia no longer took such stories seriously in 1978, and the certainty of spirits had diminished, All Saints' Day had yet to be whittled down to a minor consumer ritual or an excuse for dressing outlandishly and having a party, as it was in the rest of the United States. Halloween was still a time set aside for remembering the dead, exactly as it was for Roman Catholics in Europe and Latin America. There was a midnight mass on All Hallows' Eve. New Iberia's Catholic population took the first day of November off from work, and during the afternoon a special mass for All Saints' Day was celebrated in the cemeteries.

The earth is so damp in southern Louisiana that people are buried in crypts above ground. It was customary for relatives to put a fresh coat of whitewash on their loved ones' tombstones and crypts just prior to Halloween. Around the middle of October, hardware and paint stores began putting signs in their windows advertising "tomb paint" for sale. As Halloween drew near, the cemeteries gleamed. Every year, Catholics in New Iberia reestablished contact with the dead by tending the tombs and memories of their ancestors.

On a warm Saturday or Sunday toward the end of October, whole families turned out for a picnic in the graveyard, eating, drinking, and remembering the deceased. They gathered around the family crypts, each taking a turn with whitewash and brush, between bites of fried chicken and swallows of beer. And they did so with the certainty that when they were dead and gone, their final resting places would be the scenes of similar family gatherings.

Emmaline Broussard telephoned me at the Teche two days before Halloween and invited me out for a visit. She said she had heard that I was interested in hot peppers and she had grown them for years. I arrived at her small house in the *coteau* (Cajun French meaning rural, or outside town), and she met me at the door with beads twined around her fingers. "I was just saying my rosary, *cher*. Come right in."

She was a petite seventy-two-year-old lady with clear blue eyes and silken gray hair in a tight plait that went across the top of her scalp from one temple to the other. After more than fifty years of marriage, her husband had died a few years before. Her house had three rooms, each with clean, smooth, white-pine floorboards. She drew her own water, and on a tall wooden stand in the kitchen was an enamel wash basin. Her skin showed no sign of a tan, even though a long, hot summer had recently ended.

We sat in Miss Emmaline's bedroom on two straight-backed rockers and she told me about her life. Its mementos covered the walls: votive objects, photographs, and ornaments. Most prominent were two hand-tinted color photographic portraits, each in a large gilt oval frame. One was of a strikingly lovely young Emmaline. The other was of her late husband as a young man, with brown hair and a strong face. He had chosen to sit outside for his portrait. He was posed, stiffly, in a plain wooden chair behind the house, wearing a white shirt and beige slacks, with an iridescent brown and gold fighting cock on his knee.

Miss Emmaline told me, "I have five acres here. I've been living here fifty-four years. I could get thirty thousand if I wanted to sell it, and we bought it for a hundred dollars. Then it was really *coteau*. My old man and his uncle built this house. It cost four hundred dollars to build. We got the whole thing for five hundred dollars. Since I lost my old man, the only thing I do with this little piece of land is to let a farmer make hay for his animals. That keeps it cleared.

"My old man would look like Maurice Chevalier. Blue eyes and snowy white hair like Mister Chevalier. You talk about it—I had a good husband. He loved his birds. He had a lot of them. He always kept about thirty fighting roosters. When he died I gave away the cages. They brought back too many memories. He didn't fight the birds, he sold them. That was his pastime.

"I was just out at his grave this mornin'. Me and my friend went today to clean our tombs. We washed her husband's tomb first, then we came and washed my old man's. With about two solid hours of work, we got 'em both done. I seen a colored fellow doin' something that never hit my mind. Most people paint these tombs with a brush and some tomb paint. But this fellow was usin' a long-handled roller, and he was gettin' it done fast. Next year, if I'm still alive, I might make me some money like that," she laughed.

"I married my old man when I was just fifteen years old. And most of my girlfriends were already married by then. That's how it was in those days. I've got eight great-grandchildren. My oldest one is fourteen. I don't believe I'll see my great-great-grandchildren, but who knows? My mother has five generations. She's ninety-one and she has a good mind, too.

"My mind is still pretty sharp. In fact, I've got everything I need except for money. It's bad right now. I bought two new tires for the front of my car. Then yesterday, I blew out a back wheel. But, I like my old car. It's a '64 Rambler, and talk about a car, *cher*, that's a good one. I call it Dixie."

Miss Emmaline apologized, again and again, for her English. "When I first went to school I was eight years old, and I had never said one word of English. Today, it's still my second language. Papa didn't want us to speak it at home. He wouldn't even let me go to school before I was eight. Thinkin' I'd get hurt or something. The old folks wanted to keep us under their skirts all the time. That's why there are so many illiterate people in Louisiana."

French was not allowed on school grounds. Many people remembered receiving endless punishments as school children for letting a few French words be overheard by their teachers. This was the result of the melting-pot theory of American education, which held that the French heritage was something to be uprooted like a weed.

It did not work. Cajuns continued to speak French at home, and an overt resistance movement began in the late 1960s, when Cajuns were evincing more and more French chauvinism. Their burgeoning ethnic pride stopped short of the type of separatist movement that developed in Quebec, or the one that flourished two hundred years ago in New Orleans, but it went far enough to erase the shame that had been attached to the French language. This change in public attitudes was due primarily to the efforts of James Domengeaux, a former United States congressman. In 1968, he founded the Council for the Development of French in Louisiana (CODOFIL).

Domengeaux began by focusing the attention of his nonprofit organization on education. By 1978, there were some forty thousand students in the first twelve grades of Louisiana's schools involved in its programs. Each year CODOFIL brought scores of teachers from Belgium and France to give classes in public schools. In addition, the organization served as a liaison between many groups based in

Acadiana, profit-making and otherwise, and groups with similar interests in Europe or Quebec. This service was utilized by a number of businesses, both in agriculture and industry.

Miss Emmaline told me, "CODOFIL has a real cheap charter trip to France and I'd sure like to go. I'd love to see Paris one time before I die. But I've been poor all my life, *cher*. My old man left me a thousand dollars in the bank when he died, but Lord, I never touch that. I'm just as poor as ever. I get two hundred and eight dollars a month, but with groceries, gasoline, and havin' to pay a man to do any work that needs doin', it keeps me poor. That two hundred and eight doesn't amount to much by the end of the month."

Hard times were old news to Miss Emmaline. She was a grown woman when the stock market collapsed in 1929. People were accustomed to being self-sufficient in southern Louisiana, and much of their society was normally cashless. Barter was a common medium of exchange, so the reduced cash flow of the Depression years was not too difficult. If there was no other meat to put on the table, people were not above eating armadillo, which was plentiful and known as Hoover's hog or poor man's pig. Nevertheless, for many Cajuns those years were a daily struggle to get by and were lived perilously close to the bone.

"I remember 1931, and it was really hard times, *cher*, let me tell you," said Miss Emmaline. "I don't care what anybody says. Potatoes sold fifty pounds for a dollar, and they were little Irish potatoes. They were so small that you had to boil them a minute before you peeled the skin with your fingers. If you tried to peel them with a knife, by the time you were done peelin' there wasn't any potato left—that's how small they were.

"I remember one day a little boy came over and said, 'Please ma'am, my mama just had her baby and wants to see you.' So I went over there and she had this newborn baby wrapped in a towel because they couldn't afford nothin' else. So I went round to see my aunt, thinkin' how old people are always savin' things, always puttin' them by, and I said, '*Tante*, haven't you got a sheet or two?' The old lady gave me three, and all that night I made diapers and clothes. I took them by the next mornin'. That woman was so grateful, *cher*. I couldn't have slept that night, otherwise, for thinkin' of that new baby wrapped up in a towel."

It was during the Depression that Miss Emmaline and her husband began to grow peppers. Most people continued to buy hot sauces during those years, because it took only a little to go a long way toward spicing up a cheap, monotonous diet. It was pretty much business-as-usual for New Iberia's hot sauce manufacturers during the Depression. People who had never considered peppers as more than something to grow in their own kitchen gardens began to grow them as a cash crop.

"Me and my old man were always growin' something to make a little money. So we started growin' peppers. We had about two acres, not too much, just what we could get picked by ourselves. Lord, how I had to stay in there with the hoe when those plants were comin' up. It was a trouble to keep the weeds out. And bad on the hands when you picked it. Oh cher, that tabasco is awful! It would burn so much that I'd have to crush some ice and put it in a basin. I'd leave my hands soakin' in there for a while, then put 'em in warm milk. Go from cold to warm to try and stop that burnin'.

"We use a lot of pepper down here. When I was a little girl, there were very few people who had grinders to mash the peppers, so when they were real red we used to pick 'em and spread 'em out on a clean white cloth on a table, outside in the sun, and dry 'em. Then you would string 'em with a needle, and in every Cajun kitchen you had a big string of dried red peppers. When you wanted some, you'd wash 'em well, put 'em to soakin', and use 'em in your food. That's the only way we had.

"Of course, I always grow a few hot peppers in my garden for my own use. I slice 'em up and put 'em in things like white beans or peas. Hot peppers are especially good with pork. And in the old days, before they had cough syrups, when somebody had a cold they would make a lemon or sassafras tea and put a piece of pepper in there. They used to say that was the best thing for coughs and colds."

Over and over again, around the globe and through the centuries, these same healing qualities have been ascribed to hot peppers: they relieve coughs and congestion; they promote digestion and combat gastritis, particularly the type caused by excessive alcohol consumption; they ease aches and pains in muscles and gums when applied topically; they loosen the muscles of a tight or sore throat; and they are a stimulant.

Capsicum has been used as a medicine in the United States for many years. It was among the standard medical supplies for the Confederate and Union hospitals during the Civil War. It was applied externally for aches and pulled muscles and, as a tincture, it was taken internally for stomach distress.

When Dr. Irwin Ziment, from UCLA's Medical Center, announced in 1978 that Capsicum was useful in relieving bronchial and respiratory distress, it was reported in the press as a "discovery." Practitioners of medicine had been saying the same thing for millennia. It was only for Dr. Ziment that it was a discovery.

The human race's oldest form of health treatment is healing with plants. It is still a viable and widespread practice, its wisdom inaccessible only to those who are wholly dependent on drugs produced by the pharmaceutical industry. Capsicum is part of an age-old medical tradition as common as our humanity; it will never be outdated.

The British Pharmaceutical Codex lists it and notes that it is used externally as a "counter irritant" for the treatment of lumbago and neuralgia, and internally, in the form of a tincture, as a "carminative." A carminative is a cleansing agent, and in medicine it usually refers to something that helps expel gas from the stomach and intestines.

In addition to the list of ailments for which Capsicum has traditionally been used, there have been occasional suggestions that because hot peppers have a cleansing and stimulating effect on the membranes of the stomach, they might serve to prevent the development of ulcers in patients prone to gastric disorders. Peppers are certainly effective in treating some types of gastritis.

As recently as 1980, a whole different physical effect of Capsicum was recognized, and between 1980 and 1985 there were scores of experiments that bore out the initial findings. When capsaicin is injected into a nerve, it kills that nerve, deadening it permanently so that it cannot pass along those neural transmissions that would normally reach the brain and be translated as "PAIN." Its ability to deaden nerves is helpful to scientists studying various neural routes and systems in the body.

Researchers found that capsaicin relieved pain in rats, and they theorized that it might be of use to humans. They noted, however, that because capsaicin kills the nerve, while morphine only blocks it from receiving pain signals, injections of capsaicin are not likely to replace drugs derived from the opiate family when treating pain. Another reason that research on capsaicin as a painkiller is not being carried on in scores of laboratories is that it is not a "proprietary compound," which means it is in the public domain and a drug developed from it cannot be patented for any length of time, so a pharmaceutical company would not have a monopoly on anything it manufactured that used capsaicin as a painkiller. Without that profit incentive, there is not likely to be a lot of funding for research on the analgesic effects of capsaicin.

Nevertheless, by 1999 capsaicin was being used to treat an increasing number of painful conditions. Researchers theorized that, in addition to the capacity to kill a nerve, capsaicin worked by depleting the body's pain messenger, a protein called substance P, which is involved in transmitting pain signals from peripheral nerve endings to the brain. While the exact mechanism that causes the pain reduction is not yet clear, the effect is real and certain. Shingles, a painful form of herpes on the skin, can be treated with a capsaicin ointment available as the prescription drug Zostrix. Researchers have found that some kinds of chronic postoperative pain associated with cancer can be alleviated with a topical capsaicin cream, as can the sharp facial pain brought on by an attack of a condition called tic douloureux. Capsaicin has also been shown to reduce pain and joint inflammation associated with arthritis.

On the other side of the coin, capsaicin has a great potential for inflicting pain, and its use as a weapon and an instrument of torture has not been overlooked by either ancient or modern civilization. White men learned about this property of *Capsicum* early in their exposure to it, when the Incas burned hot peppers between themselves and the conquering Spaniards during battles. The resulting smoke was a harsh irritant that temporarily blinded the invaders.

The Mayans were said to have punished an unchaste girl by rubbing her sex with hot peppers. During the colonization of Jamaica by the British, errant Jamaicans were sometimes disciplined by having the juice of the phenomenally hot Bahamian pepper rubbed into their eyes.

Pure capsaicin was first extracted from hot peppers in 1876. As recently as 1964, the United States Army Research and Development Laboratories at Edgewood Aresenal in Maryland were conducting tests using capsaicin as a "possible non-lethal incapacitating weapon."

The capability of hot peppers to cause intense pain that passes rapidly and leaves no lasting marks makes it ideal for use in aversive therapies. People have recognized this for centuries. Mothers from the Kickapoo tribe in Mexico rub a diluted solution of hot peppers on their nipples to wean their children. A product called Nothum, marketed in the United States during the 1950s, was applied to children's fingernails and quickly trained them not to bite their nails or suck their thumbs.

Capsicum has enjoyed a great resurgence of popularity as a weapon in the United States. It is the principal ingredient in a number of brands of small aerosol sprays which citizens in urban areas carry to ward off attackers. However, since anyone can purchase these sprays, they often fall into the hands of the crooks they were designed to repel. It is not difficult to relieve someone of a wallet or purse when the person has been sprayed in the eyes with such a device. The spray causes a few minutes of total blindness. The excruciating burning of the eyes remains acute for a quarter of an hour, then slowly diminishes.

Sir John Parkinton, in his *Theatricum Botanicum*, published in 1640, mentioned that dogs hate hot peppers. The United States Post Office has issued an aerosol spray made from *Capsicum* to its carriers for protection against dogs. I knew a burglar in West Palm Beach, Florida, who always took a can of cayenne powder with him when he went to work. He would sprinkle it along behind him, claiming it served the twofold purpose of keeping him secure from canine interruption while working and safe from being tracked after his departure. Cayenne powder liberally sprinkled around garbage cans will keep canine marauders from messing with them, and powdered peppers have been used to keep deer out of apple orchards.

When the McIlhenny Company has aged a barrel of mash until it has stopped working, the mash is strained so that the husks and seeds of the crushed peppers will not wind up in Tabasco Sauce. The company sells the husks by the truckload to a midwestern pharmaceutical company, which extracts the capsaicin from them for use in a nonprescription liniment. When I spoke to Walter McIlhenny about it, he declined to name the pharmaceutical company, but admitted he thought tabasco peppers were probably good for aches and pains.

"My father used to tell me that Tabasco Sauce was far better than a mustard plaster, and thought that we ought to advertise it as such, but I don't think we ever will. A mustard plaster will literally raise a blister and burn you, whereas with Tabasco, if you take brown wrapping paper and spread Tabasco Sauce all over it and put it on your thigh, or knee, or wherever you need a plaster, it will burn like hell but it won't raise a blister, although the sensation and effect is one of intense heat. But we've always been clear about one thing: we are not medical people, we are food people, in the food business."

discovered that the business of hot sauce was conducted in much the same manner as the business of other manufactured foods. Brokers in various regions of the country acted as manufacturers' representatives. They supplied the retailers—the chain supermarkets, convenience stores, and independent groceries. Brokers not only placed the food, they went into the stores, kept track of inventories, set up advertising displays, and worked with store managers. They also supplied wholesale jobbers, called "master distributors," who placed their products in bars and restaurants.

Brokers were paid on a commission basis. This system of middlemen between food manufacturers and the consuming public had been in effect for over a century. Over the years, a manufacturer occasionally tried to circumvent the established order and sell directly to the retailers, but it was generally acknowledged that this heretical behavior involved far more time and expense than was gained by saving the broker's commission.

It was not easy to be a food broker. When salespeople called on the buyers for large supermarket chains, they usually got about fifteen minutes. In that time, they were expected to do their best to try and increase the buyer's orders for those things that the store already stocked and to sell the buyer any new items that the broker might have added to the line. Each broker represented a number of different food manufacturers, though they did not represent competing brands. Each had one line of hot sauces, one line of bean salads, one line of canned yams, and so on. Some companies, like B. F. Trappey and Sons, had as many as fifty different products. It was hard for a salesperson even to mention them all by name in fifteen minutes.

An old, established company with one well-known product was bread-and-butter for a food broker. Therefore, it was not surprising that many brokers across the country who represented the McIlhenny Company had been doing so for nearly a hundred years. Tabasco Sauce was the type of account that helped build a prosperous business. Despite the fact that it was usually the most expensive hot sauce on supermarket shelves, it sold the most bottles. For instance, on the west coast in 1978 Tabasco Sauce accounted for 80 percent of the hot sauce sold. Its widespread recognition as a quality product was responsible for introducing hot peppers to many people.

Tabasco Sauce also sold well in foreign countries where citizens had a long-standing familiarity with hot food. It was used either by itself or in addition to the whole fruit of the pepper bush. By 1986, export was responsible for almost half of the McIlhenny Company's total sales, which were estimated to have been $11.5 million.

Part of the increased demand for hot sauce in the United States came as a result of the public's changing liquor tastes. Vodka established itself as a favorite among the drinking population, and one of the most frequently consumed of all vodka drinks was the Bloody Mary. Its devotees insisted that it was not worth its vodka without a dash or two of hot sauce in its tomato juice base. Almost every bar in the United States has a bottle of hot sauce somewhere on the premises.

Heublein, Incorporated, which was the second largest liquor bottler in North America in 1978, also owned Ortega Brand chilies. They primarily marketed canned green chilies, often a relatively mild variety of *Capsicum annuum* such as serranos or anchos. These peppers grew well in southern California where Ortega had its fields. When the chilies were left too long on the bush and ripened to red, they were no longer useful for canning. Their juice was extracted and put into a product called Snap-E-Tom Tomato Cocktail, which was designed as a mixer for Bloody Marys.

There is, the world over, a strong affinity between hot peppers and alcohol. From southern Louisiana to Zaire to Thailand, it is a common sight to see men drinking and eating hot peppers. In Zimbabwe, where taverns are built in an open-air fashion with no walls and a round thatched roof, men sit in the shade, beers and bowls on the table in front of them. There are pieces of cooked meat in one bowl and small, fiery *Capsicum frutescens* in the other. The tavern's patrons take alternate bites of the peppers and the meat, sipping their beers while tears run down their faces.

In Mexico, ceiling fans turn slowly in shadowy, hot cantinas, barely swaying the strips of speckled fly paper hanging in the air. The linoleum tops of rickety card tables are pocked with raw umber cigarette burns, which hold tiny pools of cool sweat from beer bottles mixed with the warm sweat falling in drops from the brows of men orating, gesturing, and munching hot peppers.

In New Iberia, at Provost's Bar and Grill, I watched in amazement as a hefty-paunched middle-aged man ordered a plate of rice and beans and said to no one in particular, as he dashed a quarter of a bottle of Tabasco Sauce over it, "Ah been in here tryin' to eat for the las' three hours. Each time ah was fixin' to order ah'd figger to have one more bourbon and coke. Now, ah've kinda lost my appetite. What the hell?" he muttered as he shoveled in the food. "Ya gotta eat to live, right? Ya gotta eat . . . ."

Hot peppers not only complement alcohol, but they also counteract some of its negative effects on the human body. They have been used for centuries as a remedy for the sorts of stomach troubles frequently suffered by heavy drinkers. Three hundred years ago, this condition was known as drunkard's dyspepsia, and hot peppers were recommended for it in German books of herbal remedies. Today, it is more frequently called alcoholic gastritis. *Capsicum*, with its stimulating effect on the digestive tract, often helps alleviate the problem. A dash of hot sauce in a Sunday morning Bloody Mary may play as important a role in getting drinkers going again as the hair of the dog that bit them on Saturday night.

Walter McIlhenny leaned back in his chair and steepled his fingers against his chest. The ship's clock behind him chimed the quarter-hour. He spoke in deliberate, considered tones: "It is my view that the use of Tabasco Sauce in Bloody Marys is what led to its introduction into today's American kitchens. In the old days, when you asked a woman how she started using Tabasco Sauce, she would tell you that her mother or mother-in-law taught her, and that she has used it ever since. But things have changed. A mother is working during the day, and when she comes home in the evening, she and her husband pitch in and put together the evening meal with certain duties and responsibilities divided between them. We just can't count on mom to teach her daughter how to cook any more."

Unless, that is, they are a mother and daughter from southern Louisiana. Here, mothers still teach their daughters how to cook, and fathers teach their sons. In order for something to qualify as food, many Cajuns still demand more than a commodity that has been canned, frozen, or cooked in advance of being purchased. Food is more than a solution to the problem of how to get the most bulk inside the digestive tract in the least possible time with the minimum expense of effort.

The two pots most frequently found on a Cajun stove are a coffee pot and a pot of gumbo. The coffee will have been made from beans that were dark-roasted, and if it doesn't perk you up when you have a cup, you know you're dead. The gumbo is likely to have been made from damn near anything that had a little meat on its bones.

Recipes for gumbo invariably begin: "First make a roux." This is a thick, brown gravy, which has to be made slowly and with considerable care. Once the roux is ready, other ingredients are added: herbs and spices, onions, black pepper, ground sassafras called filé powder, perhaps some okra, and whatever meat happens to be available. Seafood or chicken is often used, but raccoon or possum will serve almost as well. The gumbo is frequently served over rice.

Cajuns who have gone to live in other parts of the United States speak about the experience in the same shocked tone of voice that many North Americans use to describe the privations of living abroad. Cajuns incredulously list the items that they had previously assumed to be part of every civilized person's life that were unavailable in New York or California. A Cajun, unlike most gringos, can easily adapt to life abroad without soft toilet paper, or tomato catsup, or a newspaper in English, but having to start the day with a cup of the kind of see-through coffee served in most parts of the United States qualifies as severe deprivation.

A Cajun lady of my acquaintance recounted the horrors of her exile from Louisiana. She had married a man from Massachusetts, whom she had met while he was working in the oil patch. He insisted they go back to New England and set up their household. She did so, although it was against her better judgment.

"Those winters and that snow, *cher*. That was bad enough, but what I really missed was my grits and coffee in the mornings. When I went in the grocery store up there and asked for a box of grits, they didn't understand me. Like I was speaking a foreign language or something. They had never heard the word before! Grits, I told them, grits, and they asked me what grits were. I had to explain it to them. I couldn't believe it. I still can't believe it," she said, shaking her head.

She convinced her husband to give married life in Acadiana a try, and now he would not live anywhere else. While she told me this story in her living room, her three children arrived home from school. The youngest, age seven, told her he was hungry. She said, "Go in the kitchen and get yourself something to eat. You're old enough to help yourself."

The child took a long time in the kitchen. We heard the rattle of dishes, the scrape of a chair being pulled up to the stove, the creak of the kid climbing on it, then the liquid sounds of pouring and spilling. Finally, he reappeared in the living room, precariously balancing a bowl of gumbo and a cup of coffee, which looked to be about half milk. He sat down and polished off both. His mother beamed at his precociousness and told me the gumbo was made from blackbirds she had shot the previous day in her front yard. She said that being so small had made them difficult to clean, but worth it, as they had proven quite tasty.

When I met her, Dr. Patricia Rickles was a professor of folklore at the University of Southwestern Louisiana in Lafayette. She was a middle-aged, heavy-set lady with a surprising grace and lightness to her step, and she had one of the best collections of Cajun folklore in existence.

Her classes were always full to overflowing. After many years of teaching it, she was still excited by her subject, and she communicated that excitement to her students, many of whom had never heard the word folklore before they took her course.

The great majority of her students were Cajuns. State universities were free to Louisiana youngsters who had graduated from high school. Increasing numbers of them were choosing to attend college. They were the first generation to receive their folklore in the classroom rather than from their elders at home, but their parents had become too Americanized to pass on the old knowledge. Professor Rickles was engaged in salvaging a cultural heritage that might otherwise have been lost. It was no surprise that she was able to excite her students and capture their interest. She was giving them their birthright. Her folklore files continued to swell as class after class went out and interviewed parents, grandparents, relatives, and neighbors.

After more than twenty-five years in Louisiana, Patricia Rickles still professed astonishment at the amounts of hot pepper people used in their food. "I'll admit that I come from a bland culture. I'm a native of Wyoming and we were never big on eating, but it utterly boggles my mind to this day. I have learned to enjoy Cajun seasoning, but my God in heaven!"

She laughed. "There was a student of mine, a little bitty wiry boy, who used to ride quarter horses at the racetrack in his spare time. He quit because he said it was too dangerous. Not the riding, but the spectators. He told me, 'Cajuns'll kill you if you lose a big race.' He wouldn't ride any more. Anyhow, my husband and I were having a crawfish boil, and he said he would cook the crawfish because he was a real, dyed-in-the-wool coon-ass."

A coon-ass? She digressed from her story for a moment. "I have not heard an etymological explanation for the term which satisfies me. I do know that it has nothing to do with the pejorative term, coon, that is sometimes used to refer to black people. Wherever it comes from, the Cajuns have proudly assumed it. The more respectable, non-Cajun element deplores it, of course. There is a bumper sticker that reads: 'Coon-asses make better lovers because they'll eat anything.' That's a pretty strange thing to say about yourself. I know a forty-eight-year-old Cajun wife and grandmother who has that on the back of her car.

It's sort of like giving the finger to the world. Very French, it seems to me. I love it. It's as far from WASP attitudes as you can get."

She resumed her story: "Anyhow, this ex-jockey came and he fixed an extremely hot crawfish boil. He put in large quantities of cayenne. It was all I could do to eat those crawfish, but they were delicious. Your mouth and lips got numb after a while and you could enjoy it. Then he asked, 'Has everybody who is not a coon-ass had enough? Now, the coon-asses will eat.'

"He brought out a jar of cayenne that was a foot high, dumped it on top of what was already in there, and cooked the crawfish. He threw in whole unpeeled Irish potatoes, and they absorbed some of that pepper. You could cut one open and it would be red all the way through. People ate that with real relish! I've eaten in Mexico, but I've never seen anything like that."

Hot peppers, in most cultures, have always been fraught with sexual symbolism and associated with the sex organs. Acadiana was no exception, as Dr. Rickles's files of folklore showed. At the turn of the twentieth century, young men went so far as to sprinkle the dance floors with cayenne, in the belief that when the powder rose among the dancers, the young ladies would be aroused and unable to resist their partners' advances with the usual Catholic ardor.

Professor Rickles told me, "I heard a story twenty years ago from either Vivian Washington or Teresa Guidry. I forget who told it to me, but I remember the story to this day. Both ladies were black, middle-aged, rural Catholics. The lady in question had worked at Avery Island as a young girl, picking peppers. She was not allowed to come into the fields during her menstrual periods, because it would draw some of the heat from the peppers. During her monthly, she was on her honor to stay home from work. I don't know who decreed this. Surely none of the McIlhennys, who were very educated and sophisticated. I presume it was either a Cajun, a black, or a work-boss of some kind."

Regardless of who promulgated it, this stricture was closely tied to the ancient taboo against women having intercourse during their menses. The shape of red peppers, plus their redness and heat, have traditionally linked them to male sexuality. In seventeenth-century European botanical medicine, *Capsicum* was under the dominion of the planet Mars.

During the Kingdom of the Sun in Peru, Incan warriors preparing for battle were required to abstain from sexual intercourse and from eating peppers. As recently as 1970, the Peruvian government announced that hot sauce would no longer be used in prison food, because it tended to arouse sexual desire in the male inmates and was therefore "not appropriate for men forced to live in a limited lifestyle."

In Swahili, red peppers are called *pilipili hoho.* The word *pilipili* is also slang for penis. Remarkably, *pilipili* means the same thing in the slang of Cajun French. There is, in fact, a variety of *Capsicum annuum,* occasionally grown in Texas, that so closely resembles the male reproductive organ as to be universally monickered the "penis pepper." Almost every botanist I spoke to who specialized in *Capsicum* would go for a laugh sometime during the interview by saying, "Get a load of this," and reaching into the far back corner of a desk drawer to pull out a penis pepper.

There is something to be said here for the doctrine of signatures: the belief that plants indicate how they are best used by some sign such as shape or smell. *Capsicum* is often recommended in the old herbals for complications of the male genito-urinary system, particularly those problems that accompany old age. Whether hot peppers are of real benefit in treating those problems is a question that awaits scientific inquiry, but it is certain *Capsicum* can provide a level of sensory excitation that becomes increasingly harder to find as one grows older.

In addition to being specifically equated with male sexuality, hot peppers have been perceived, for centuries, as exacerbators of desire in both sexes. People around the world have labeled them as aphrodisiacs. For some, this quality was attractive and for others it was reason to shun the peppers, but people have long regarded peppers as sexual stimulants.

As early as 1600, Father Joseph de Acosta addressed the subject in his book *The Natural and Moral History of the Indies:* "When this Axi is taken moderately, it helps and comforts the stomacke for digestion: but if they take too much, it hath bad effects, for of its self it is very hot, fuming, and pierceth greatly, so as the use thereof is prejudicial to the health of young folkes, chiefly to the soule, for that it provokes to lust."

During the 1600s, while the use of *Capsicum* spread across Europe and throughout the world, the Puritans forbade the use of all spices, considering them to be excessively stimulating to the body. They categorized peppers as being among the worst offenders. At the other end of the world, the Chinese contemporaries of the Puritans in the provinces of Hunan and Szechuan came to the same conclusions about the aphrodisiac quality of peppers and began using copious quantities in their food, believing such stimulation to be beneficial to their health.

Among the three lower castes of Hindus in India, lust is expected and excused. The dietary regulations applying to these people condone the use of hot peppers,which are avidly consumed. They are forbidden, however, to the Brahmans, members of the highest caste. Brahma is the universal primal energy incarnate, the creator of all things. Brahmans must strive toward purity, and they do not eat *Capsicum*. Adolescents of the Brahman caste, during the potentially volatile period between puberty and marriage, are urged to practice *bramacharya*. This is a regimen of keeping oneself pure, of conquering desire and conserving vital energy.

In his book outlining the principles of *bramacharya* for young Brahmans, Swami Narayananda gives the following advice: "Avoid taking too much of the chilies or any food that causes bad feelings, sense irritations, or heats the system. The food that produces too much heat in the system makes the blood and sexual fluids watery and the mind restless; thus one becomes subject to lascivious desires, thoughts, wet-dreams and seminal disorders."

Oh yes? Well, there are certainly some advantages to being born impure, unsaved. The laughter of the lower castes, enjoying their peppers, comes faintly to the ear, and fades slowly like smoke.

 was introduced to boudin (pronounced *boo-dan*, with a nasal inflection) at a bar and grill called Paul's Place. I had stopped in for a late afternoon beer. The middle-aged lady behind the bar, who had faded red hair and circles under her eyes, told me, "I've been working here near twelve years. That's a long time. My Paul is a sick man. Somebody's gotta do the work for him. He's got sugar diabetes, ulcers, and heart trouble. It's too bad, but what can you do? He just hasn't been well for a long time."

I said I was sorry to hear it.

"He went down to our camp this morning. He likes to go down there and do a little deer hunting. We had a cup of coffee before he left. He had just took two of his five-milligram nerve pills, instead of the usual one. He was feeling pretty good. Real calm. He gave me one of those Equanil this morning too, and I had a few drinks on top of it this afternoon." She giggled like a schoolgirl.

She went into the kitchen and brought out two fat links of pale, thin-skinned sausage on a paper plate. "Here," she said, setting the plate down on the bar between us. "Have some boudin. I'm sorry this is the last of it, or I'd offer you more. Seems like no matter how much of it I bring along to work, it's all gone by the time I get ready to go home."

Boudin is a delicious Cajun specialty, a dressing made of rice, pork, onions, hot peppers, and spices, which is stuffed into a casing made from a length of hog's intestine. It is served warm, and most markets keep a crockpot behind the counter full of *boudin*. Homemade *boudin* occasionally has blood added to the stuffing, but markets are allowed to sell only "white" *boudin* to the public. Blood *boudin* is a treat that cannot be bought with money.

A hog butchering in southern Louisiana is called a *boucherie*. As for many of the world's pork-eating peoples, it is a festive occasion. There is a considerable amount of labor involved in slaughtering a hog, and what better way to entice family and friends to lend a hand than to make a celebration of it? It is, of course, desirable to use as much of the hog as possible, and the Cajuns do a good job of it. Traditionally, at a *boucherie*, the men are responsible for butchering the hog and making the deep-fried pieces of pork rind called cracklings. The women make the *boudin*, measuring the ingredients by eye, using recipes that have been handed down to them for generations.

Wilda Moran took me to my first *boucherie* on a hot Friday morning. We drove from the offices of the *Daily Iberian*, where she had worked as a reporter for nine years. She was in her early forties and had spent most of her years with the newspaper covering Acadiana's agriculture and industry. In the process, she had studied these two fields in depth, and she was a knowledgeable observer of the changing economy in Iberia Parish.

The occasion for the *boucherie* was a fund-raising dinner to be held the following Sunday by the Knights of Columbus. Seven hogs were being butchered for the dinner. The slaughtering took place out in the *coteau* behind a church called Our Lady of Prompt Succor. Sunday's meal would be served in the recreation room of the same church, following the morning's religious service. One of the Knights had called Wilda to see if she would come out and do a story for Saturday's paper, in hopes of initiating a last-minute flurry of ticket sales. The meal cost only $2.50, and promised to be well worth the price.

Wilda was glad for a reason to get out of the office and into the countryside. She liked to be out among the citizens, and she was always ready to lend a hand for anything she considered a good cause. She had lived all her life in Iberia Parish, and she knew a remarkable number of people there, from poor to powerful, by their first names. She was an unabashedly aggressive born-again Christian, exuberant without being self-righteous, a stocky woman with a hearty laugh and a palpable zest for life. She had been attending *boucheries* since she was an infant.

"I can remember how it was done when I was little. The men making the cracklings would dump that hog rind into huge three-legged iron pots, and after a while all the fat would be melted out of it. They would be standing out there stirring it with big boat paddles, while the women were in the kitchen doing the rice, and the *boudin* dressing, and everything else. You would take a dishpan full of the stuffing, and you'd have a bunch of guts already prepared—cleaned and salted—for the casings. You had a gourd funnel, and you would slide a casing over it and go to stuffing the *boudin* through the funnel.

"My dad was a sugar cane farmer. We were poor, although I didn't know that until I got to high school. It always seemed like we had enough, though we were sure not to let anything go to waste. I remember when I got married in 1950, my dad butchered a hog and a calf. He cooked huge roasts outside in those big black iron pots. The day before the wedding you could smell it for a mile away in the breeze. To have that kind of meat offering for guests was real status! My dad was somewhat taken with his one and only daughter, bless his soul."

A cat ran across the road. Wilda Moran reacted quickly and swerved, narrowly missing it. "Thank you, Jesus," she murmured.

In the old days, her father would hire a score of migrant workers for the eighty-day cane harvest in his fields. Her voice was full of nostalgia as she remembered it: "I can just see it now. It is a warm autumn evening. I am a little girl, looking at one of my father's cane fields being burned and harvested. The flames are burning bright and gorgeous. In those days you did not have the tractors and trucks to carry the cane out of the fields like you do now. There were mini-trains, called 'little dummies,' that traversed the cane fields. I can still hear the sound of that little dummy, and see it in the background as it's crossing the field, just chugging along through all that smoke and fire.

"Behind me, my mom is cooking standard fare on a big four-burner wood stove. The meatballs were the size of a softball. Two of them were apt to do the trick. And there's also a tremendous pot of white beans. Rice, meatball stew, and white beans. The workers would get this twice a day for however long they stayed. The beans would begin to disintegrate and form a cream, and on top of it are floating onion tops and peppers. Hunks of salt meat. Then, the oven would be full of baking sweet potatoes. And the aroma! Oh Lord, the aroma!

"There was a large building on the back of our land, and two or three tiers of cots would be hung on each wall. That's where the workers would stay. I didn't realize it then, but it couldn't have been too pleasant for those people. It didn't have any plumbing, for one thing. But my folks certainly kept everybody well-fed. I'm telling you, we had enough garden to feed an army."

By the time we reached Our Lady of Prompt Succor, it was already late in the morning. The men were almost through with their butchering. The seventh and final hog lay decapitated and disemboweled on the back of a flat-bed truck. A handful of men were working. Some cut up carcasses with hacksaws, while others brought out steaming pans of boiling water to pour over the mottled pink and white flesh of number seven, so the bristles would be easier to scrape.

The Knights of Columbus had been working since dawn. When this last hog was finished, they would knock off for a while, then return with their wives to make the cracklings and the *boudin*. Wilda asked a tall older man in a denim workshirt, "*Tu as fini?*"

He grinned. "*S'approche.*"

We were offered beers, although it was only eleven in the morning. Wilda turned the offer down, but I could not refuse it under the hot sun, surrounded by flies and the smell of hog's blood. A substantial number of empty Dixie cans were lying around and a collection was being taken up for another couple of six-packs. The men were wearing bloody aprons and their arms were gory up to their elbows. In the background of our desultory conversation was the steady scraping of a broad, flat-bladed cane knife, shaving the hard stubble from the pigskin.

The man in the denim shirt laughed and asked, "How we gonna get all the publicity we need when the dinner be day after tomorrow? Where you been hidin', Miss Wilda?"

Another was quick to say, "Never mind him, Miss Wilda, you know he's just kiddin'. We're all mighty grateful that you came on out today."

A third man told a joke, which I heard repeated half a dozen times during my stay in bayou country: "You know the definition of a real

Cajun, Miss Wilda? It's a man who can stand and look out over a field of rice and tell you how much gravy it's gonna take to cover it!"

Wilda told one back: "You know what makes a seven-course Cajun meal? A bowl of gumbo and a six-pack!"

There were constant cries for more hot water. The man in the denim workshirt opened a fresh beer for himself and handed one to me. He struck up a conversation. "Where are you from?"

I told him.

"Well, ah knew you wasn't a coon-ass with a name like yours. People in your part of the country probably don't all come out like this when they got a few hogs to butcher, right? Down here, folks get together for one of these *boucheries*, and everybody works hard as hell, but we all have a good time. We've already sold a thousand tickets to the dinner. What is it that brings you down here?"

I told him. He laughed. "Hot peppers? Well now, ain't that somethin'? That's a damned good money crop, those peppers. Ah'll never forget one time when ah had a fella here from Oklahoma that had come to help mah company buy up some land for a right-of-way. Ah took him out to show him the land, and we passed a pepper field on the way. He asked me, 'How does anyone make a livin' growin' peppers?' When ah tole him what folks were gettin' for a hundred pounds of peppers, he decided he might be interested in buyin' a piece of land and raisin' some hisself.

"He got so excited about it that I thought he was gonna wet his pants. Nothin' would do but for me to stop the car right there so's he could get out and have a look at that field. Well, ah'll be damned if the first thing he did wasn't to reach out and handle a pepper, then go to rubbin' his eye a few minutes later without even thinkin' about it. Whooee! Right then and there he decided he didn't want anything to do with peppers, but it took him quite a while longer before he could stop cryin'."

The last hog was scraped clean and hacksawed in two. The pair of slabbed ribs were put up on hooks to hang alongside the others. The sight of the morning's porcine carnage had not, apparently, diminished any appetites. The men began to drift off in their cars and pickups, heading for their noonday dinners. Wilda asked me if I was hungry. I admitted to it and she suggested we get something to eat before she returned to the *Daily Iberian*.

She drove back by way of the Acadiana Regional Airport and Admiral Doyle Drive. We stopped at a franchise steak house located squarely in the middle of the hamburger stands and convenience stores that lined the highway. The place was a cafeteria, offering a choice of steaks to be served on a platter with a baked potato. Plastic daisies were in white vases on each table. There was a typical American lunch-hour crowd of attorneys and engineers wearing ties, and enclaves of well-dressed secretaries.

"I can remember when there was a sugar cane field right here," Wilda told me. "It could have been bought fifteen years ago for a few hundred dollars. It staggers the mind! Even the land nobody wanted because it was so poor, nothing but *coteau*, even that is selling for seven or eight thousand an acre. Speculators are having a heyday around here."

Wilda Moran's articles in the newspaper were always pro-industry and pro-agribusiness, but she acknowledged that the boom economy had produced a number of casualties. "I've watched the pepper industry go down, down, down in these parishes. There's still a little pepper picking being done, but it's not the kind of work that most people are willing to do these days.

"When you're out in the pepper fields you've got to work stooped over, and those peppers eat through the flesh. For many years sugar cane was cut by hand, but it was never so hard as picking peppers. In sugar cane today, people walk behind the mechanical planters and straighten the stalks in the furrows. You do this with a cane knife, and not your hands. It's no picnic, but it's a lot easier than working with the peppers. Then, too, it's an hourly wage, whereas peppers is piece-work."

Even the sugar cane industry felt the pinch for labor when the boom was in progress. The cane mills paid only minimum wage, and starting pay in the oil patch was almost half again as much. The turnover at the mills was tremendous. Many of the owners complained that as soon as employees gained any expertise with dials, gauges, and gears, they left to find jobs in the petroleum industry.

"Things have gotten so bad during the last four or five years, the mills have begun to take in women," Wilda said in 1978. "When that starts happening in the cane mills, you know there's a real labor shortage. Before that, women worked out in the fields, behind the tractors. Now they're on the mill floors and they are out in the yards and they are running the front-end loaders and all of that other equipment."

*

When oil prices dropped, labor shortages ceased to be a problem at the mills, but women would not willingly give up their jobs to return to field labor, nor could they simply go back home to resume the role of housewife and raise their families. It was too expensive to raise even a small family when only the man was earning a wage, to say nothing of how hard it became when that man found himself out of a job. In the old days, when people fished, farmed, trapped, and built for themselves, when money was a luxury and not a necessity, a woman's day was full of the work to be done to keep a family of ten, fifteen, or twenty kids on an even keel, as well as helping her spouse with whatever task might need another hand. The children themselves were not simply passive recipients of nurture and support, but contributed their own labors to the daily routine, and there were plenty of chores to keep them occupied for most of their waking hours. There was wood and kindling to be gathered, fields to be weeded, and fish to be cleaned. Children did not hang around clutching at their mothers' skirts and whining for something to do.

For children in the consumer society, there is only television and hyperactivity. Even those women who are willing and able to stay home all day are less and less willing to accept the traditional Cajun notion of a large family. Three children in late twentieth-century America are more than enough to send a young mother out seeking pharmaceutical relief from stress and anxiety. An informal survey that I took of New Iberia's pharmacists confirmed that a large number of prescriptions for Valium were being written and filled for young housewives in Iberia Parish.

As gender roles and the concept of family were redefined, the Catholic Church lost a degree of credibility. The use of contraceptives among Louisiana's Catholics is generally agreed to be widespread.

The Church's vision of a harmonious and procreative marriage is out of tune with the realities and difficulties involved in raising a large family. The Church became fallible in the eyes of its members, and its ability to support unquestioning faith began to erode. The loss of a firm religious grounding provoked more anxiety and further recourse to Valium. This syndrome has been common in the rest of the United States since the Second World War, but it was only during the 1970s that it surfaced in Acadiana.

Southern Louisiana males, who liked to think of themselves as the self-satisfied, hard-living patriarchs of large families, were particularly ill-equipped to deal with a change in what they considered a woman's place in their lives. Individual relationships between men and women frequently became strained as the culture made its adjustments. These men were beginning to learn that the money market is a game you have to pay to play, and that the price can be as high as the affections of wife and daughter or the sacrifice of an untroubled belief in the possibility of eternal life. In Louisiana, men were beginning to sense a loss of control, and their efforts to regain it seemed puny and impotent. The Church refused to condone birth control, and the state legislature refused to ratify the Equal Rights Amendment, but these things did not change the fact that women were demanding changes on many fronts, and were going to get them.

One hot afternoon, visiting people who lived at the edge of a cypress swamp, I was introduced to a twenty-year-old woman who had three children. She chain-smoked and her fingernails were bitten down to the quick. She told me her own mother had had twenty children, all of whom had lived to adulthood. She added that many of her mother's friends had raised families the same size.

"Twenty kids! Can you imagine it, cher? Twenty kids? I just got three, me, and they're too much to handle. All day long I'm either shouting viens ici or trying to keep them out of my hair. Never a happy medium. Just three, and I have to take my nerve pills every day just to keep up with them. And my mama raised twenty of us. She died last December and I know she must surely be in heaven this very moment."

II : THE SALT MINES

t has never been easy to make a living as a farmer. Long hours, fluctuating markets, and living in constant fear of crop failure due to disease, weather, or acts of God have often combined to make farmers old before their times. Yet prior to World War II, there was always a significant number of Americans who chose to farm. To work one's own land is, after all, as ancient an ambition as agriculture.

This choice of livelihood has become a financial impossibility for members of the lower and middle classes in the United States. Farmers who worked small plots of land have been systematically wiped out by the combined efforts of agribusiness, the federal government, and agricultural colleges. Each of these monoliths has contributed to shaping an American agricultural policy that supports only the largest and most impersonal of farming operations.

The trend has been for a few large farms to replace many smaller ones. From 1950 to 1980, over 3 million farms disappeared. Large farms have not led to the crop diversity one might have expected. Instead, the huge tracts of land are usually planted in one crop which can be farmed and harvested mechanically. This kind of homogeneity has yielded high, short-run profits, but over the years it has taken more from the ground than it has given back. The soil has become undernourished, loose, and unproductive. Wendell Berry, in his extraordinary book on American agriculture, *The Unsettling of America*, described this as "extractive" agriculture.

This extractive approach bears a marked resemblance to the manner in which America's petroleum resources have been removed, and it is therefore not surprising to find that agribusiness firms and oil companies are often owned by the same groups of investors. In fact, modern farming techniques represent an astonishing triumph for the petroleum industry. Not only are gas and oil required to run the machinery, but fertilizers, pesticides, and herbicides are manufactured by chemical companies which are often owned by petroleum corporations, and fossil fuels are used extensively in the manufacture of many animal feeds.

Wendell Berry writes: "That we should have an agriculture based as much on petroleum as on the soil—that we need petroleum exactly as much as we need food and must have it *before* we can eat—may seem absurd. It *is* absurd. It is nevertheless true."

Hot pepper growers were limited in their ability to apply agribusiness techniques to their crop primarily because of the difficulties encountered in developing a profitable mechanical harvester. Even before the recent advances in mechanical harvesting, however, the petroleum industry had managed to insinuate itself into the pepper fields in a number of ways, and reliance on things like chemical fertilizers, herbicides, and pesticides had greatly increased.

There was little doubt, in 1980, that a mechanical pepper harvester was on the horizon, but there was also little doubt that it would be designed for the larger varieties of peppers such as those grown in the Southwest. Even without such a machine, the pepper growers in California and New Mexico were producing record numbers of chilies. In Texas, more and more acres of jalapeños were being planted and picked each year. These states were close to the Mexican border and had a reliable supply of cheap labor. By the end of the century, a pepper harvester that worked on chilies was indeed developed and was in widespread use in the Southwest.

Southern Louisiana was not so fortunate. The possibility was very real in 1980 that hot peppers would soon cease to be grown in Cajun country on a commercial basis, with the exception, perhaps, of a few token acres on Avery Island—and by 1999 this was exactly the case.

One ironic facet of this situation was that the market price for hot peppers had never been higher. In 1978, a grower received forty-seven cents for a pound of tabasco peppers, and an acre could be counted on to produce about eight thousand pounds. That was a gross income of $3,750 for each acre grown.

"Why, sure it's good money! It's damned good money," W. J. Trappey shouted at me, outrage quivering in his voice as he swung forward in his swivel chair and brought his feet down on the floor with a bang. "That's what I'm trying to tell you. And cayenne is good money, too. It's bigger, easier to pick, and usually yields around twenty-five cents a pound. A farmer who grows a hundred acres of cayenne or tabasco for me, and gets it picked, is gonna make a lot of money. If he can get it picked. But it doesn't do to have those peppers out there and not be able to get them harvested."

New Iberia's hot sauce manufacturers generally viewed the disappearance of people willing to do field labor as a result of the laziness and willfulness of the poor, combined with the devastating effects of federal laws governing equal opportunity employment. W. J. Trappey believed that if the federal government would stop its meddling, the workers might yet return to the fields.

"This town has completely changed over the last few years. We've gotten some of these do-gooder types, you know? Groups that are funded by the federal government. Looks like their primary purpose is to take field hands who they figure are underpaid and make every effort to get them off the farm and into industry. The government supplies funds to these people who have taken this thing on like a mission!

"It used to be that people would work because if they didn't, they went hungry. Now nobody's hungry. They learn the ropes of the system and can sit home making as much as if they were out there picking peppers. I've watched it happen in every field."

Walter McIlhenny blamed the scarcity of field labor on the oil industry. "There are many, many people whose capabilities limit them to driving a tractor or working in the fields, but they don't want to do this work any more. They want to be welders, pipefitters, or electricians. And they just don't have it. They just can't hack it.

"That's what is upsetting the economy of this area. The people who have been in agriculture now refuse to do that work, and this forces agricultural activity out of the area. The day will come when Americans are going to be in a bind because nobody wants to work on the farm. We'll be getting our tomatoes from Mexico and our beef from Argentina, and this country will no longer be self-sufficient. The time will come," he intoned, making a gloomy, military assessment.

*

In the '70s, as big money moved into southern Louisiana, big government followed close behind. To be on the map is, after all, to join the nation. When one listened to the middle-class white men in New Iberia, however, it seemed as if the federal government had targeted Acadiana for an experiment in doling out injustice and abuse. Nowhere outside of deep Dixie were citizens so vitriolic in their denunciations of Washington, D.C. Cajuns have been voting for the Democratic Party in local elections since Lincoln won the Civil War, but many of them haven't voted for a Democrat in a presidential election since Roosevelt won his first term.

Despite the invective against Washington's bureaucracy that was such common conversational currency, New Iberia was deeply dependent on the federal government. The United States Coastal Zone Management program funneled over a hundred million dollars a year into southern Louisiana. Federal money paid a substantial portion of the costs incurred when the Port was deepened and widened. A grant from the Department of Housing and Urban Development (HUD) enabled the city government to refurbish New Iberia and to build a block-long parking lot to serve downtown businesses. Another HUD grant was responsible for finally getting asphalt pavement on most of the blocks in the southside section of town. And, of course, there was the federal government's subsidy of sugar cane prices, with which no one quarrels.

Even with these blandishments of largesse, the marriage of Acadiana to the rest of the United States was not easy to bring about. There was constant tension, and, in a manner characteristic of many bad marriages, it often erupted into arguments that were never fully resolved but only added to a deepening reservoir of grievances. While I was there in 1978, I saw an example of how Louisiana had cooperated with the federal government on a project that had the potential to become a serious liability to the state.

After the Arab oil embargo of 1974, the United States Department of Energy (DOE) decided to stockpile a billion gallons of crude oil as an emergency supply. Eighty percent of this oil was scheduled by the DOE to be stored in five huge salt domes, like the one beneath Avery Island, along the Gulf coasts of Louisiana and Texas. One of these storage sites was at Weeks Island, where the Morton Salt Company had formerly operated a mine. Weeks Island is less than twenty miles from New Iberia, and is connected to it by Highway 83 and the Bayou Teche.

There were accusations that in order to get state and parish permits for the oil storage at Weeks Island, including permission to cross the ecologically delicate Atchafalaya Basin with a thirty-six-inch pipeline that would carry oil from St. James on the Mississippi River, the DOE had agreed to consider underwriting a further deepening and widening of the Port of Iberia channel. This would have allowed the largest class of supertankers to navigate the channel. The DOE claimed these improvements might allow the Port to act as a backup system in case the pipeline should malfunction. The DOE laid out $300,000 to help pay for the necessary environmental impact study on the project at the Port. Permission was given to the DOE for its pipeline. The pipeline was laid, but nothing beyond the environmental impact study was ever done to make the plans for the expanded Port a reality.

"We're still waiting," said Port director John Oubre in a bitter tone, as he sat in his office at a slumping Port of Iberia in 1986.

The first site chosen to begin actually storing the federal government's oil was a salt dome at West Hackberry, Louisiana, some 120 miles west of New Iberia. The DOE billed it as a showcase for their new program, although some Hackberry residents questioned the wisdom of pumping oil out of one place in order to pump it back into another. In fact, one town official characterized Hackberry's participation in the program as a "shotgun wedding" with the DOE.

On September 22, 1978, while workers were routinely going over a hole drilled in the Hackberry dome, a spark ignited a geyser of oil and it immediately burned out of control. Flames shot thirty feet into the air and the cloud of smoke could be seen from Houston. One man was killed and another badly burned. It took five days before the fire could be put out.

A deputy project manager for the DOE was quoted as saying that the accident showed the safety of salt mines for oil storage. He pointed out that if a similar fire had happened at an above-ground storage site, where tanks were being used, the resulting explosions would have been much more devastating. Governor Edwin Edwards took strong exception to this line of reasoning. He noted that the DOE had specifically assured him that such a fire was one of the things that could never happen. He added that he was investigating the possibility of suing the DOE for damage to the environment of Hackberry.

The furor quieted. No suit was filed and the DOE continued with its plans for oil storage. It is hard to blame the government for finding the salt mines a tempting place to store something as precious as petroleum. Five hundred feet into the earth, in a mammoth vault made of rock salt, seems about as safe as you can get. So safe, in fact, that the mines drew the attention of the multitude of people who needed to find a safe place to store the nation's rapidly increasing volume of nuclear wastes.

During 1978, Union Carbide Corporation conducted a heat evaluation program in the salt mines beneath Avery Island to help determine if such a site would be a feasible place to dump the radioactive garbage that must be deposited somewhere it can stay while it deteriorates for the next half million years or so. The tests consisted of nothing more than drilling three holes into the floor of the mine and inserting electrical elements to heat the surrounding rock salt to five hundred degrees. Engineers watched to see if the salt cracked, expanded, melted, or was otherwise affected. What was surprising was not that Union Carbide thought it could simulate the effects of a half million years of degenerating nuclear wastes, but that the McIlhennys let them use Avery Island to do it.

"We have done everything we could to assure that nothing will be stored in the mine," Walter McIlhenny said. "We rejected the idea of storing oil here. And that wasn't the first idea we had rejected. In the fifties, when there was a lot of unrest in the country about nuclear attack, the salt company wanted to store microfilms in the mine. I wouldn't allow it, and the reason is that you might get a bunch of dead-end kids who thought we had a second Fort Knox here with gold and jewels, and that we were only saying it was microfilm. Then they'd come out here and raid the place, fifty or a hundred of them, and tear it up. I did not care to be subjected to that, so there was no microfilm stored in the mines."

*

The salt domes are the result of a geological process that took about 180 million years. First, a large ocean that covered what is now the Gulf Coast evaporated, leaving a sheet of salt. This was eventually buried under fifty thousand feet of sediment. Pressure accumulated beneath the sediment and caused portions of the salt layer to rise in giant columns. There are two hundred fifty such formations along the Gulf Coast, but only five, including Avery, Weeks, and Jefferson Islands, ever broke through the earth's surface. Avery Island is the highest of the five.

Life was first attracted to these prominent hills of salt over nine thousand years ago. Beneath Avery Island soil, many well-preserved bones of prehistoric animals have been found. The first sloth and tapir remains found on this continent were discovered there. Sixteen feet below the surface, a mastodon skeleton was found, along with evidence of saber-toothed tigers and three-toed horses.

Human beings are known to have been on the island as early as 1500 B.C. Pottery shards found around the briny springs by the salt mines suggest that Indians of the period harvested salt from the deposits. Scholars theorize that two groups lived on the island, but many came to stay for a little while and gather salt, both for their own use and for trade.

Curiously, by the time white settlers arrived in 1760, the indigenous Atakapas (pronounced *attack-a-paw*, now extinct) were extremely reluctant to visit the island and preferred to go elsewhere for their salt. They told the white men that a catastrophe, the exact nature of which they never revealed, had occurred on Avery Island. They considered it a place of sorrow and ill fortune.

In 1896, only a little more than thirty years after the Yankees had destroyed the island's saltworks, H. S. Kneeder wrote of the sophisticated salt mining operation he had seen there, which was being carried on at a level of 180 feet, in a mine 1,400 feet long. Nearly a century later, I descended to the 700-foot level, and by 1998 the mine extended down more than 1,200 feet. It was estimated that the salt ran to a depth of 50,000 feet, but for safety reasons the plans were to stop mining when they reached a depth of 5,000 feet.

The salt was loosened by explosions, just as it was in 1896. Holes were drilled fifteen feet into the walls of the mine, and the last five feet were packed with ammonium nitrate explosives. Ammonium nitrate is more difficult to detonate accidentally than dynamite, which was the explosive of choice in Kneeder's day. When the ammonium nitrate was fired, the wall blew outward, and upwards of two thousand tons of salt could be recovered after each explosion. In 1985, the mine produced about 2 million tons.

The only source of illumination in the mine was an occasional bare bulb shining through the haze of salt that hung in the air. There were three underground transfer stations at different levels, where the salt was cleaned and crushed. At the deepest of these, five hundred feet down, an electromagnet removed the metallic impurities from the rock salt as it flowed by on a conveyor belt. The transfer stations were massive complexes of belts and machinery as large as Ferris wheels, strung with bare bulbs. Old lengths of worn-out belts and pieces of antiquated machinery lay abandoned in piles on the floor of the mine. They could lie there, perfectly intact in that dry air, for thousands of years.

At that time, the mine was over a mile in length and consisted of huge chambers, often a hundred feet high. Floors, walls, and ceilings were all 99 percent pure rock salt. The mine was much the same at seven hundred feet as when Kneeder described it at the 180-foot level in 1896: "Beneath one's feet the white salt crunches like frost. Far off in black depths the ruddy tapers of the miners twinkle, and the figures dimly moving about are like gnomes busy with some supernatural task. It is weird and spectral, the spectral spirit of Dante, and the weird legends of the Inferno."

12 : GENETICS

considerable amount of research has been done on the genus *Capsicum* over the last thirty years. As with almost every known genus of flora and fauna, academic careers have been built around its study. Even Tabasco Sauce has been taken into the laboratory. Scientific research has established, among other things, that the sauce has a freezing point of minus five degrees centigrade; its exact color is Brazil Red #3; and the average bottle contains 7.8 percent of that volatile chemical, capsaicin.

Much of the information gathered about *Capsicum* has proved more immediately useful. Many varieties are now known to cross-pollinate quite readily. If a hot *Capsicum annuum*, like a cayenne, is grown within a mile of a milder variety of *annuum*, like a bell pepper, there is a good chance the seeds from the hotter pepper will produce a fruit that is considerably milder than its progenitor. Hot sauce manufacturers cannot afford to receive this kind of surprise from a field of peppers that they are counting on to produce barrels of mash.

Both Trappey and Bruce Foods, New Iberia's second and third most widely known makers of hot sauce, depend on cayennes and jalapeños. Unlike cayennes, jalapeños do not lose their piquancy when they hybridize, but their size begins to vary, and this was another deviation the companies found unacceptable. It was almost impossible to find a location to grow peppers in Louisiana or Texas where there would not be at least one other *annuum* growing close by. Both companies were buying their seeds from seed companies, which grew their plants in high-altitude fields in Colorado or California where there was no risk of cross-pollination, and distributing the seeds to farmers in Louisiana or Texas who grew the peppers for them.

The McIlhenny Company did not need to have its seeds grown by an outside company. Although *Capsicum frutescens* will cross-pollinate with *Capsicum annuum*, it shows little inclination to do so, and Avery Island was far enough away from any place where other tabascos might be growing. It was necessary, however, to provide the company's Latin American farmers with seeds for the tabascos they would grow. Numerous varieties of *Capsicum frutescens* abound south of the border, and the McIlhennys could not take a chance of getting anything other than the variety which their customers knew and loved.

Each year, as the peppers began to ripen in the Avery Island fields, the president of the company walked through and tagged the plants that would be used to produce seeds. Farmers in Latin America were bound by their contracts to plant only the seeds sent to them from Avery Island.

Scientists from Louisiana State University's Department of Horticulture were able to show the McIlhennys how to increase the germination rate of their seeds from 15 to 90 percent. It had been a tradition on Avery Island to store each year's seeds in an attic, where temperatures often reached one hundred degrees Fahrenheit. When the company began packing their seeds in nitrogen and storing them in a cool place, the rate of germination soared.

The ease with which *Capsicum* cross-pollinates is both a bane and a blessing to botanists. There has been some innovative work done in experimental breeding. Dr. Roy Nakayama, a professor at New Mexico State University, was one of the pioneers in the field. In 1975, for instance, he bred a chili pepper that was disease resistant, could grow to a foot long, and weighed a third of a pound. He named the pepper Numex Big Jim, in honor of a local farmer who had worked closely with him. Pickers found the Big Jim to be ideal—easy and painless to pick. Its only drawback was a low heat level, around a three on a one-to-ten scale.

The search for disease-resistant hybrids has received substantial amounts of support from the pepper industry. This is not surprising, considering the 20 percent annual mortality rates in the field from diseases. Dr. Walter Greenleaf, a professor at Auburn University, bred a variety of tabasco pepper in 1970 that was resistant to tobacco etch virus. The pepper's resistance was the result of a hybridization with *Capsicum chinense*, during which the two were crossed over twenty times. Dr. Greenleaf's research was supported in part by the McIlhenny Company, which asked only that in the event of success he not use the word "tabasco" in the name of his hybrid. Despite the fact that the small *frutescens* is universally referred to as a tabasco pepper all over Louisiana, the McIlhennys have a legal right to the name as a proprietary one. The generic use of the company name was a sore point, and this was made quite clear to Greenleaf, but the temptation for the professor was, apparently, irresistible. He named his creation "Greenleaf tabasco." The McIlhennys do not grow it.

*

There are numerous difficulties in developing a standard taxonomy for *Capsicum* because of its ability to cross-pollinate between species. The problem has occupied a number of botanists. Two whose work is well known and respected are Dr. Paul Smith from the University of California at Davis and Dr. Charles Heiser of Indiana University, in Bloomington. Each has worked on the taxonomy of *Capsicum* for over twenty-five years.

Dr. Heiser and a former student, Dr. Barbara Pickersgill, published a taxonomy of cultivated *Capsicum* in 1966 which became the generally accepted version. It accounted for five species of domesticated hot peppers: *Capsicum annuum* and *Capsicum frutescens*, with which North Americans are familiar; *Capsicum pubescens*, which is commonly cultivated in the high Andes of Peru; *Capsicum baccatum*, which is found in many South American locations at mid-altitudes; and *Capsicum chinense*, which is grown near sea level in South America and the West Indies.

These five species did not make up an inflexible list. It was considered likely that new species were still to be found and named. After all, the bulk of flora in South America was still unknown to botanists and remained to be identified. In some remote location, no doubt, people were growing a pepper that was uncatalogued: some pepper bush that was not quite a weed or a cultivated plant, but was tolerated and occasionally encouraged to bear fruit.

When I visited Dr. Heiser, he showed me a pepper from Peru which he suspected might be a previously unrecorded wild species. Indiana University seemed an unusual place to view anything so exotic. Bloomington is a long way from the highlands of Peru, and even a considerable distance from the flatlands of New Iberia.

I went to Bloomington during the first cold snap of the year, passing steep hills and winter woods of thin trees with bare branches jutting up to the gray sky. The road led first through Gnaw Bone, then on to Bloomington. Students were bundled up, and their breath made smoke signals in the cold air.

Dr. Heiser's new pepper was keeping warm in the tropical air of a large greenhouse on top of the building that housed the Department of Plant Sciences. Dr. Heiser was a tall, rangy, balding man. He was dressed in cowboy boots, a sport shirt, and slacks. His belt buckle was a large, ornate silver and turquoise oval. He was proud of his new pepper from Peru. Although it was less than a foot tall, he assured me that within sixty days it would bear bright orange fruit that would be short and hot.

"Twenty-five years ago I described another new species from South America, called *Capsicum cardenaseii*. This is a wild pepper which is sold in all the markets of La Paz, Bolivia, and has been there for many years. Someone bought these peppers back from the market and it turned out they had never been described."

Capsicum cardenaseii grows wild. People harvest its fruit, but they do not truly cultivate it. The same was true for the Peruvian pepper in the Plant Sciences greenhouse. Most experts would not even hazard a guess as to the number of wild or semi-wild species of hot peppers growing in the world. Many of the differences that can be observed between species of the cultivated plant become blurred in the wild. Because three out of the five cultivated species—*annuum, frutescens,* and *chinense*—will hybridize, they are believed to have come from a common wild ancestor.

"There is no problem in classifying the other two cultivated species, *pubescens* and *baccatum*, as separate," Heiser said. "*Pubescens* will not hybridize and *baccatum* will only produce sterile hybrids. But some would say that *annuum*, *frutescens*, and *chinense* are one species and others would say three. The plants do not have closed gene pools, so although scientists aren't supposed to say such things, it becomes somewhat arbitrary whether they should be called species or subspecies."

Capsicum is a plant that defies fixed borders, historically and genetically. Dr. Heiser concluded that primitive peoples were aware of the tendency of *Capsicum* to cross-pollinate. "Many of the Indians in the Amazon, for instance, are careful cultivators. I saw people growing different pepper plants in carefully separated places. To me, they were all just hot, but these people wanted one sort in one dish and a second sort in another dish. They grow these as perennials for many years. Occasionally, a seedling will come up which they'll recognize as a hybrid, cultivate, and eventually find a new use for in their food."

The uncertainty about which hot pepper should be classified in what species has resulted in squabbling between botanists that has continued unabated for centuries. In the mid-eighteenth century, Linnaeus designated *Capsicum* as the name for the genus, and recognized two cultivated species. By 1832, botanists had enumerated more than twenty. Then, in 1898, H. C. Irish made the bold move of reducing the number to two. In the mid-1920s, L. H. Bailey set a record low by reclassifying the entire genus into one species. Since that time, the number has begun rising again.

In addition to being unable to agree conclusively on a standard number of species, botanists have engaged in numerous academic disputes over the names of individual varieties. This is a matter of preeminent importance to many scholars, although the shelf life of a varietal name seems to be less than a century. These arguments are carried on in journals with names like *Baileya*, *Phytologia*, and *Taxon*.

Botanists who specialize in hot peppers have spent a lot of time over the last twenty years engaged in breeding experiments that attempt to combine genetic traits and produce a hot pepper that is both disease resistant and adaptable to mechanical harvesting. These are the kinds of experimental agendas that might well motivate a hot pepper aficionado familiar with agribusiness methodology to visit some Louisiana pepper fields under cover of darkness and steal a few cayennes or tabascos for their seeds. When universities and agribusiness take aim at a particular fruit or vegetable, anything can happen, including the disappearance of that particular taste from the flavors available to the human palate. When more and more of a given crop is raised on huge tracts of land under exactly the same conditions, using precisely the same amounts of fertilizers, herbicides, and pesticides, and planted with genetically engineered seed stock, there is a real possibility that the food, as humans have known it, is in danger of vanishing from the world's larder.

For a number of years there has been concern among people working in botany and agriculture that many ancient genetic codes—in the cells and seeds of our oldest foods—are threatened with extinction. Not that there won't still be something called "wheat" or "tomatoes" or "corn." But the seeds from which these things have grown will have been genetically engineered to maximize profits, and the seeds for these plants as our fathers or grandmothers or, in some instances, our prehistoric ancestors knew them will no longer exist. They will have been entirely replaced by a strain of plant developed to fit agribusiness farming techniques and production goals.

The National Seed Laboratory in Fort Collins, Colorado, is the seed bank for the United States. It is there that the seeds from endangered species of plants are deposited for safekeeping. As of 1979, the laboratory had not received a single budget increase from the federal government in fifteen years, despite the fact that those fifteen years had produced an unprecedented number of genetically manipulated fruits and vegetables.

The problem is serious. Garrison Wilkes of the University of Massachusetts has written: "Suddenly . . . we are discovering Mexican farmers planting hybrid seed corn from a midwestern seed firm, Tibetan farmers planting barley from a Scandinavian plant breeding station, and Turkish farmers planting wheat from a Mexican wheat program. Each of these classic areas of crop-specific genetic diversity is rapidly becoming an area of seed uniformity."

In his comments on this passage, Cary Fowler from the Rural Advancement Fund in Wadesboro, North Carolina, wrote: "Seed companies, governments, and international agencies have gone into areas where traditional varieties predominate and promoted the new plants, often calling them 'miracle varieties.' Convinced of the 'superior' qualities of the new variety, the Third World farmer or peasant ceases to grow the traditional crop. Instead leftover seeds of the traditional variety may be used as food for the family or their animals. In a moment's time, thousands of years of crop development and seed selection become meaningless, and another variety becomes extinct."

This trend toward uniformity, a hallmark of agribusiness, has potentially grave consequences. If an unlooked-for infection, infestation, or blight should wipe out a genetically engineered plant, and the seed stock of its progenitor has been lost or allowed to become extinct, the survival of that food in the world would be seriously jeopardized. National Academy of Science figures demonstrated the extent to which the United States had become dependent on genetic conformity in 1980: three kinds of millet made up the entire United States crop; two kinds of peas made up 96 percent of the crop grown; and four kinds of potatoes comprised 72 percent of the American crop.

Hot peppers are also threatened. Among the descendants of the Maya, for instance, some of the world's longest users of hot peppers, traditional seed selection techniques are being discarded. It was an ancient obligation among fathers to provide seeds to the members of their families at the beginning of the planting season. During each harvest, patriarchs set aside the seeds for their families to plant during the following year, and they used all the care that the patriarch of the McIlhenny family uses when he performs the same annual task. The seeds of maize, beans, calabash, and hot peppers, the staples of the Mayan diet, have always been selected in this manner. Recently, however, due primarily to logging operations conducted in many of the Mayan communities, money has begun to circulate among local residents, and the younger generation has taken to purchasing seed in the local tienda.

Among industrialized Western nations, the attack on hot peppers has been more sophisticated and insidious. Legislation in Europe and the United States has made it possible to patent newly bred varieties of fruits and vegetables. The rationale for such legislation was that it would encourage agribusiness to carry on research for "more productive" genetic strains, since they could patent, and therefore profit from, any new strains they developed. In the United States, this type of legislation was first passed in 1970, and it was called the Plant Protection Act. Although hot peppers were not covered in the original act, *Capsicum* was among six foods added to the act in 1980.

It is not hard to understand that if only one sort of seed is being used to grow the majority or even the entirety of a given food crop, and if that seed is exclusively owned, the potential profits for the patent owner are enormous. Within ten years after President Nixon signed the Plant Protection Act in 1970, there were more than one hundred corporate takeovers of American seed companies. In England, one week after similar legislation was passed, one corporation acquired eighty-four seed companies. In other European countries, multinational conglomerates have taken over many of the nationally based seed companies and are busily applying for patents on a wide variety of genetically manipulated plants.

Seed companies became highly attractive investments. Sales of seeds to government programs and agribusiness, both at home and abroad, guaranteed a reliable market. People have to eat, and seed companies were flooded with offers of corporate acquisition. Few were prepared to turn down those large offers. Bye-bye Burpee Seed Company. It was bought by General Foods. Ferry-Morse came under the aegis of Purex. And oil companies were certainly not going to miss out on a good place to invest capital—you could bet your socks on that. NAPB (Olin and Royal Dutch Shell) acquired Agripro, and Union Carbide bought Keystone Seed Company.

Under the Plant Protection Act, the cost of a seventeen-year patent for a life form was originally set at $750, but by 1986 the actual cost of taking a new variety through the application process was over $2,000. Gary Nabhan, a research investigator at the Arizona-Sonora Desert Museum in Tucson, wrote: "This severely limits what small seed companies, amateur breeders and growers, and others can breed and even grow. On the other hand, breeders backed by agribusiness can manipulate one or two genes in an ancient variety, then patent and 'own' a complex of genes that was actually selected over thousands of years."

Multinational corporations profit from genetically engineered seeds in much the same way that they profit from petroleum in a place like southern Louisiana. They take what they can get for as much profit as they can, with little regard for the people or environment from which they are extracting their profits. Most of the seed stock of our planet has its roots in the southern hemisphere, in those places that now make up the Third World. Often a multinational corporation will genetically engineer a new strain using that stock, which they will then turn around and sell to Third World farmers or governments in the countries where the seed's progenitors originated. By 1998, things had moved well along their sinister way. Varieties of grains and vegetables were being developed with a suicide gene. When a plant was mature and ready to be harvested, it was genetically programmed to release a poison that killed the seeds in the plant so they could not be used again and new seed would have to be bought.

Food, including hot peppers, is being systematically removed from the control of the general public and put in the hands of specialists. A direct relationship between citizens and what they eat is beginning to be circumscribed by law, distancing food production yet another step from "the consumer"—an extension of the process that started with agribusiness driving small farmers in the United States from their land.

*

One morning in the New Iberia library, a young black man sat down across the table from me with a copy of *Rolling Stone*. He was thin, with a scraggly mustache and goatee. He seemed tightly wound, and I could feel his intensity across the table. Despite the warmth of the day, he was wearing an Army greatcoat, which he kept on in the library. A casualty.

When he struck up a conversation with me, his voice was soft but tinged with urgency. He asked me who I was and what I was doing there.

People who strike up conversations with questions about who you are usually want to tell you who they are. His name was Donald, and he had been born and raised in New Iberia. He saw eighteen straight months of combat in Vietnam and had not been the same since he got back in 1971. He had not been able to stay in school or hold a job.

"My nerves have been real bad ever since I got back. They gave me nerve pills, but I don't like to take them because I can't think clear on them. But my nerves have been bad. *Real bad.* When I got back I registered to take a degree in political science over in Lafayette. I wanted to find out what was really behind the war and all. You know, I *really wanted* to find out. But I couldn't study. I'd try to concentrate and wind up thinking about the stuff I saw over there.

"I get a monthly check from the government. I can't hold a job 'cause I can't concentrate no matter how I try. So I live on that government check. Sometimes I try to make a little more working at Avery Island during the picking season. I did it just last week, but I couldn't work there for no more than an hour and a half. It has gotten to where it hurts my hands too much. Man, those peppers burn! I worked just that little time, only made six dollars, but my hands burned all day and kept me awake all that night."

Donald told me his family used a bottle of Tabasco Sauce a week, and that he liked to chop up whole tabascos to use in his food. He added, "I've got a few pepper bushes of my own growing in my mother's front yard. They're from Avery Island seeds. Most people I know who have worked there took a few peppers away with them for the seeds. What harm does it do? They're just using those peppers for themselves, growing them in their own gardens."

 have always been a walker. It is how I prefer to get around, and it did not take me long to notice that New Iberia was a hard town on pedestrians. A car, preferably big and fast, was one of the primary components of an individual's identity in Acadiana. Not only was driving regarded as an inalienable and God-given right, but anyone who did not choose to get behind the wheel when given the opportunity was viewed with suspicion. Old and young leaned out of their auto, van, or pickup windows to yell at my walking self as they sped past. It may be that their yells stemmed from the fact that I was a stranger with a somewhat swarthy and Levantine complexion, but I think it was probably just simple disdain for a human being on shank's mare that caused teenage boys to give me the finger and grown men to shout "Hey asshole!" at me as they drove by.

In October 1978, the first marathon run ever held in Acadiana was put together by the combined efforts of some joggers' clubs and civic groups. The twenty-six mile course wound through Iberia and Lafayette Parishes. Much of the race was cross-country, but there were occasional stretches where the runners were routed alongside the road. As with most such events, the participants were a mixture of local running enthusiasts and professionals who traveled the country entering such marathons. The Sunday of the race was a warm day with a slight breeze. Fine running weather. When the pack of runners reached the portions of the course beside the highway, they were repeatedly "buzzed" by cars, trucks, vans, and motorcycles. One runner was injured when a motorcycle struck him on the leg. The professionals said they had never witnessed anything like it. One participant remarked that the hostility of the local citizens had made it more like fighting a war than running a race.

*

Alan Daigre had been the mayor of New Iberia since 1964. When I interviewed him in 1978, he was a heavy man in his early sixties, with dark hair combed slickly back from his forehead. He wore a heavy pair of black-rimmed glasses that would have looked more at home on a *yeshiva* student riding a New York City subway. Mayor Daigre's broad face was pock-marked and jovial, and he had a politician's wide smile.

"We don't have a comprehensive land-use plan," he told me. "We use spot zoning. It may not be the best, but it has served our purposes. In 1959, the city developed a comprehensive zoning plan that never went into effect because it was never adopted by the people. In that plan we had all the property around Admiral Doyle Highway set aside for future residential areas. Now that land has become highly commercial. We are just letting property go its own way and develop as it will. We're going to let land use take its course as the city develops. So far, it has handled itself pretty well."

This *laissez-faire* attitude toward land-use planning was held by most of the region's local politicians, and it created the potential for some serious environmental problems in Acadiana. There was some inadequate sewage treatment as a result of too many people and too few treatment facilities, and there were a number of reported cases of cholera before things were finally put under control. With haphazard city planning, there are likely to be serious environmental concerns that do not get addressed during periods of rapid growth, and this was a problem for a while in New Iberia. After the oil boom, when everyone had pretty much gone back to wherever they came from, the threats to the region's environment still primarily came from oil, but they were no longer related to a boom-town economy.

Large oil spills presented an ever-present threat to the ecologically fragile marsh and swamplands of southern Louisiana. Some marine biologists believed that when oil was absorbed by a marsh it did not disappear but was gradually released back into the environment from the sponge-like marshes, resulting in significant long-term damage to the life that thrived there.

The Atchafalaya Basin covers 440,000 acres of Acadiana. Much of the Basin is swampland, which is flooded in the spring by the Mississippi River. The flooding begins in late February and lasts until early summer, with the water level in the swamp ranging from about five to fifteen feet. By summer's end, the swamp is usually dry ground again, although the Atchafalaya River flows through a part of the Basin year round.

Even during the dry season, there are numerous backwaters and bays formed by the river in the Basin. Each of them has tiny tributaries and channels that lead away from it back into the swamp. These little fingers of water are frequently choked by the floating green and lavender blossoms of water hyacinths. The hyacinths multiply extraordinarily rapidly, and can actually suffocate a small body of water or an entire bayou, making solid ground where there once was water.

As recently as a hundred years ago, gigantic first-growth cypress trees grew in the swampland of the Basin. It was some of the hardest wood in the country. In the first ten years of the twentieth century, logging companies went in and dragged out all of the ancient trees. The roads they made doing so can still be discerned during the dry season. The narrow tracks look like scars of barren ground as they wind through the dense creepers, vines, snake lilies, and other swamp vegetation. Nothing has ever grown back where the huge logs were dragged by men and mules from the deep swamp to wherever there was enough water to float them. Twelve-foot-wide cypress stumps still stand among the tupelo gum trees and the second-growth cypress. It is not a fast-growing tree: the second-growth cypress, seventy years later, is only a foot or so in diameter.

There are a multitude of ways to make a living from the Basin. Musk-rats abound in the swamp, and trapping them has always been a re-liable source of income. Thanks to M'sieu Ned McIlhenny's insatiable naturalist's curiosity, nutria are now more plentiful than muskrats, and their pelts fetch a good price.

In the old days, moss picking helped augment many an income. Spanish moss was gathered off the trees with a long pitchfork and sold to local moss gins, where it was processed for furniture makers to use as stuffing. The traditional boat for working back in the Basin was the pirogue, a canoe hollowed out from a cypress log. A pirogue was the ideal swamp boat because "it could float on a heavy dew," but it has generally been replaced by flat-bottomed wooden boats that have a motor mounted on the stern and a steering wheel built in near the bow. These models also draw remarkably little water.

There were also plenty of catfish and buffalo fish in the Atchafalaya. In the fall of 1978, catfish were selling for forty-five cents a pound and buffalo for fifteen cents. A good-sized blue catfish, the true chan-nel catfish and the one most commonly caught, averages around four pounds. When the swamps flooded in the spring, the crawfish season began. The man who fished for catfish when the ground was dry would then spend his time in the swamp setting crawfish traps, underwater around the tree bases where the crustaceans liked to gather. A good day during crawfish season could bring in a few hundred dollars.

Clifton Charpentier was a man who made his living from the Atcha-falaya Basin. Short, with a Cajun's big thick arms and broad chest, he had reddish-blond hair going to gray and hugging his head in short, curling tufts. He was clean-shaven, and had small, bright blue eyes. In his early fifties, he smoked a couple of packs of Winstons every day. He had short hands and stubby fingers which were overlaid with cal-luses. He had been wresting a living from the Basin for only four years. Before that he owned a construction business and suffered from stom-ach trouble.

"An ulcer? I'm tellin' you, man, I had a *bad* stomach, me. More than one ulcer. I had to give up eatin' things like hot peppers. Then I started fishin' for a livin', gave up the construction business, and I haven't had a bit of trouble with my stomach since. Now I can eat anything I damn well please."

In the autumn, when the swamp was dry, he fished for catfish in the backwaters of the Atchafalaya River. A string of three hoop nets was laid out, with the nets about twenty yards apart. Each one had a bag of old cheese in it to act as bait. The fish swam through a narrow opening in the hoop to nibble at the cheese and could not find their way back out again.

The day I spent on the water with Clifton Charpentier was extraordinarily pleasant. He was kind and patient, explaining his work and gently remonstrating when I got in the way of his efficient one-man operation. He gave me certain small tasks, like filling the bait bags, so I was able to feel useful.

"I always fish alone," he told me. A lot of guys have a partner. They figure it's worth splittin' the money so there'll be someone along to talk to and help out, but I've always liked workin' alone. It's only bad if you hurt yourself. I've broken a few ribs since I started fishin'. The last time was during crawfish season. I was comin' back after a day in the swamp and the boat hit a cypress knee. Threw me into the gunwale and I broke two ribs. Didn't bother me too much. I went home, saw the doctor and he taped 'em for me. I went back out the next day. Had to. Crawfishing is a seven-day-a-week job. They're not going to be there very long, so during the season you don't take any days off."

He had one of those flat-bottomed boats with motor and steering wheel. It was sixteen feet long and carefully designed. The bow was covered. Between the steering wheel and the two-compartment fish box, which took up most of the aft portion of the boat, were four feet of open space. This was where he worked and where he was likely to spend his whole day. He told me a story to illustrate how rarely he finds himself in the back of the boat.

"In the springtime, when I'm workin' the crawfish, the water moccasins are comin' out of hibernation. They like to get up in the trees back in the swamp, drape over the branches, and get warm in the sun. When I go after crawfish, I get up against those trees and sometimes one of those snakes will drop into the back of my boat. I just leave 'em there till the end of the day, then I take my paddle and flip 'em over-board. But *cher*, if the wife is along I have to kill 'em right away. The wife hates snakes."

When I went out with Clifton, we were on the water by 8:30 A.M. The sun was bright and warm. There was a slight breeze and only a few wisps of cirrus clouds high in the sky, which disappeared as the morning wore on. We started off with a fifteen-minute boat ride down the Basin. The water was muddy brown and appeared to be treacher-ously shallow in spots. There were places where herons were standing in the middle of the current on their thin, stalk legs. Huge bars of silt were lying just under the surface. Small islands, overgrown with thin willow trees, were numerous.

The Atchafalaya Basin used to be covered with water. Now it is mostly dry land. The reason is that the United States Corps of Engi-neers has been successfully practicing flood control for the last fifty years. Before that, it was not just the back swamps of the Basin that flooded in the springtime. During the worst years, farms and towns would be inundated as the Mississippi overfilled every body of water in the area.

The last big flood was in 1927. Emmaline Broussard, who lived over a mile from the Bayou Teche, remembered when the levee broke in '27 and she went into her front yard with a pirogue tied on a line around her waist. She caught crawfish and put them in a bucket in a pirogue. She kept the boat tied to her front porch for a week.

The Corps of Engineers brought severe flooding under control, but the water level in the Atchafalaya Basin suffered. "In my daddy's time, this Basin was fourteen miles wide," Clifton told me. "Now you can see across it. The Corps built their levee after the flood of '27, and now the siltation here is out of control. The water moves so slowly that the silt builds up, and then you get those scraggly willows, and what you've got is another patch of useless land where it used to be water. I hate those damned willows."

He began to recognize some private set of landmarks and knew that somewhere close by was the spot where he had set a string of nets two days before. He slowed the boat to a crawl and tossed out his hand-made three-pronged iron grappling hook on its long length of rope.

With his right hand on the steering wheel, he passed over the area two, three, and four times. Finally the rope in his left hand went taut. The grappling hook had snagged his line of nets. He killed the engine and began to haul the nets alongside.

The first net reached the surface and the water suddenly boiled with the thrashing of fish. He wrestled it up over the gunwale and dumped it onto the four feet of deck space, then pulled a broad shovel from under the bow, and shoveled the fish into his fish box, buffalo in one compartment, catfish in the other.

There were fifty buffalo fish and four catfish. Since the latter was worth three times the former, he was not too happy with the contents of the net. The buffalo are large, flat fish, pink and gold flounder-shaped carp that range between two and six pounds, with the gristly, toothless hole of a carp's sucking mouth. Their scales flashed rainbows as they flopped about on the wet gray deck of Clifton's boat.

"When these buffalo fish get in the net they thrash around, and I think all that commotion keeps the catfish away. When you have a lot of buffalo in a net, you're never goin' to have a lot of catfish in that same net."

The second net on the line was also full of fat, flopping buffalo fish. Not one of the sleek, silver-blue, scaleless catfish in the bunch. He began to haul in the third net on the line and knew by the feel of it that it held a different story. He finally dragged it alongside and I gave him a hand hauling it in. As he had guessed from his tug on the line, the net was full of catfish. They ranged from twenty-two down to eight inches. There were only three buffalo fish in the net. He smiled as his shoveling began to fill the catfish side of the box. "That's two hundred pounds of catfish. Ninety dollars worth."

It was 9:30. The sun was just beginning to get really warm and Clifton had already paid for his day. Everything to come would be gravy. In the course of a day, he would hoist and reset three lines of nets, each with three or four hoop nets on it. He decided to reset these in the same place, so he put in fresh bait bags and tossed them back in the water.

We motored across toward the far shore. Then it was back out with the grappling hook until he found his second line and pulled in the nets. Three loads of buffalo fish. When the last flopping fish was shoveled into the box, he closed it and sat down on the wooden cover to smoke a cigarette and tell me a story.

The previous spring, during the middle of crawfish season, somebody had begun robbing his traps. For days in a row, they came up empty. He knew that even bad luck never rode a body that hard, so he gave up his precious work time and staked out a set of his traps. For two days he hid in his boat behind a growth of cypress and watched. On the evening of the second day, the thief appeared in a wooden skiff just like the one in which Clifton was sitting, stiff from waiting in the cooling air.

"I watched him out there robbin' me. I knew him and he knew me. After I watched him go around and clean out the traps I pushed my boat out and showed him my face. Asked him how it was goin'. Some nerve he had. He said, 'All right, but not as good as yesterday.'

"I said, 'You know what you're goin' to do with those crawfish, don't you? Give 'em to me, 'cause they're mine, that's what you're goin' to do with 'em.' He saw my pistol sittin' right there on the deck. But I had been thinkin' about what I was goin' to do for two days. I knew I wasn't goin' to hurt him. If I'd come across him doin' it, and not had time to consider the situation, I might have gotten violent. I'm glad it didn't happen that way, me.

"He handed those sacks of crawfish over. I told him, 'I want you to think about this while you're paddlin' home,' and I reached into his boat and cut his gas line. You know that was one tired thief by the time he paddled his nine miles home."

Thievery was a minor problem for Clifton, but it was worse in the northern part of the Basin near Baton Rouge. In the main channel of the Atchafalaya, fishing can be a mean business. There are problems with things like "shockers." These are boats that drag a line in the water behind them through which a live current is passed. It spreads out through the water and electrocutes fish. Those with air in their bladders when they die float to the surface. This will comprise about a quarter of the fish in any given area. The other three-quarters sink to the bottom where they will never be harvested. If the electricity passes through a fisherman's net, he pulls up a load of bloated corpses. Instead of the thrashing of a hundred fifty pounds of struggling, sentient fish, there is nothing but dead weight.

Thieves and shockers are not, however, the biggest threat to those who earn their livings from the natural bounty of the Atchafalaya Basin. Siltation is a bigger problem. Another is that parts of the Basin, including the one where Clifton fishes, are crossed by a thirty-six-inch pipeline built to carry oil between Saint James and Weeks Island. Swamps are delicate webs of land and water, fine fragile balances that are capable, for all their delicacy, of supporting a great variety of life. One large leak into the Basin could wreak havoc on its ecology for many years.

The idea of applying land-use planning to the Basin had certainly not been ignored, but there were a lot of different uses of the land envisioned. Interested parties had put forth their proposals, but a consensus had not been reached. The Corps of Engineers had recommended that the federal government take over the Basin and restrict or prohibit fishing, trapping, and agriculture, while preserving it as a wilderness area. This idea met with considerable resistance from citizens and parish police juries.

The land was primarily in the hands of private owners. A small amount of it belonged to people like Clifton Charpentier, who maintained a houseboat camp down one of the numerous waterways that led into the swamp. When the weather was nice, Clifton and his wife packed up and left their ranch-style home to spend weekends at the camp. Clifton had built the houseboat himself. It was small, clean, and comfortable, serving him as year-round headquarters for his fishing business, as well as a storage place for his bait and equipment.

Most of the land in the Basin, however, was owned in huge holdings by agribusiness corporations, which wanted their land kept dry and above water at all times. They cleared the timber and planted soybeans or rice or whatever they could grow for the best money. The monstrous tracts of land, which once teemed with life, subsequently supported nothing but a few workers, a single crop, and machinery—huge combines with headlight eyes that moved through the fields around the clock.

In 1976, the state of Louisiana took a step that appeared to support these agribusiness interests: it was decided to prohibit permanent dwellings in the Atchafalaya Basin. When Governor Edwards announced the state's plan, Clifton Charpentier was outraged.

"That was too much for me. These people would do harm to this place that nobody who lived here would ever think of doing. We are the ones who really know this Basin and give a damn about it. That's when I met Governor Edwards," he laughed. "We got forty-four thousand signatures on a petition in three weeks' time and took it to him. I'm a hard-headed coon-ass when it comes to it."

He got no argument from me. It took a hard-headed coon-ass to give up his own construction business when times had never been better for builders. He had given up talking on the telephone, wheeling and dealing; no more driving from place to place with a CB radio in the pickup and tension in his stomach; and no more giving orders to employees or taking them from clients. Instead, he was doing a young man's work—lifting, hefting, and shoveling—and doing it by himself.

t was my last morning in New Iberia and, as is often the case when one is on the verge of leaving a place, my thoughts dwelled on the future. I was sitting in a cafe, eating my last meal in Acadiana, but in my mind I was already in New Orleans: having a drink at Lafitte's Blacksmith Shop; walking the elegant avenues of the Garden District under the night light of a moon coming full in Taurus; or listening to Professor Longhair moving people to dance with his boogie-woogie piano at Tipitina's Club on Napoleon Avenue.

"You the fella writin' about hot peppers?"

I looked up from my oyster poorboy to nod, and saw that the strong bass voice belonged to a short, stout man with a shock of white hair. He was wearing wire-rimmed spectacles, and behind them his blue eyes were strong.

He extended a blunt liver-spotted hand for a firm handshake. "George is my name. If you don't mind I'll bring my breakfast over here and tell you what I know about 'em," he said, eyes drifting across my sandwich, thinking, perhaps, that someone who would be eating an oyster poorboy at eight in the morning might prefer to be left alone.

I quickly invited him to join me. He got his more orthodox breakfast of coffee and biscuits and carried it to my table, balancing the plate of biscuits on the coffee cup without a tremor. The waitress brought us refills for our coffee and he told me a bit about himself. His parents had come to New Iberia from Shreveport, in the northwestern part of the state. Although he had been born in Iberia Parish, he made it clear that he did not consider himself a Cajun, because there had been no Acadian blood in the veins of his parents.

"Neither my momma nor my daddy ever cared much for hot peppers, but I've always been crazy about 'em. My younger sister never took to 'em, but I think that was 'cause one day when she was a kid she got into a bunch of tabasco peppers that were growin' in the yard next door and got it in her eyes. What a racket she set up! Screamin' and screamin'. The neighbor women came over and stood around chatterin' in French. Then they took her inside and laid her down on her back on top of our kitchen table and poured some cane syrup all over her face and hands. In a few minutes my sister was sittin' up eatin' a piece of candy like nothin' had happened.

"I can remember when I was little how I used to watch men as old as I am now eatin' hot peppers. Cayenne and tabascos. Stuffin' 'em into their mouths and drinkin' beer to wash 'em down. I'm no Cajun, but I love the hot stuff. I make a hot sauce that's better'n anything the McIlhennys ever put on the table, if I do say so myself. I just don't think I could take much pleasure from eatin' if I couldn't have hot food."

Anthropologists have begun to pay an increasing amount of attention to what people eat. Much can be deduced about a culture from its diet. The things that people will not eat and the things they consider essential to a meal reveal many dimensions of their lives, beliefs, and values.

The Minanghabau in western Sumatra are a good example. They are avid consumers of *Capsicum*, both *annuum* and *frutescens*. When they begin to fall ill, to feel not quite right, to come down with something, as it were, one of the first things they do is stop eating peppers. When they take them up again there is a general sigh of relief among relatives over the individual's return to good health. The Minanghabau have created a relationship with peppers that defines, for them, the state of their health and, therefore, the quality of their lives.

People all over Indonesia have deep respect for hot peppers as a primary food and eat them daily. The Malay word for a sauce made with hot peppers is *sambal*. There is a common sauce called *sambal ulek*. *Ulek* means "mashed fine," and the recipe calls for small, fiery *frutescens* to be mashed in a stone mortar with a stone pestle. A little fresh lime juice is added and the sauce is ready to serve, brimming with heat and vitamins.

This same preparation is known all over southeast Asia. In Thailand, it is called *nam prik*, and it is an integral part of a Thai meal. It is used in a wide variety of ways, some of which border on the bizarre. Dolf Riks, a restaurateur in Pattaya Beach, described one: "Sometimes a part of the male 'meang dah' beetle is added to *nam prik*, and then it is called *nam prik meang dah*. The male beetle has a delicious perfume, something like Chanel No. 5, and the female thinks the world of it. When incorporated in *nam prik*, the beetle makes it very special."

People all over the world get their daily doses of vitamins A and C from hot peppers. In addition, people place a high value on the sensory stimulation peppers offer, and they pity Europeans and North Americans who cringe from hot food as though it would do them harm, and who adamantly refuse its pleasures.

The idea of measuring one's health and quality of life by one's relationship to hot peppers is an idea that Clifton Charpentier put into practice. He sought a manner of earning a living that did not put stress on his stomach, one that would allow him to eat what he wanted when he wanted. Maalox was not sufficient. The search had to be carried on outside the realm of antacids and pharmaceutical nostrums. Deeper solutions, such as giving up a business and finding a more satisfying occupation, had to be considered.

Until recently, almost the only places in the United States where people had this kind of kindred feeling with hot peppers were southern Louisiana and the southwestern states. In those regions, rich and poor alike considered hot peppers part of their daily lives. The peppers were easy to grow and, in the Southwest, there were often plenty of the wild *chiltepin*, or bird peppers, which needed only to be picked and eaten. In other parts of the country, this attitude did not prevail. A few folks could always be found who were growing *Capsicum* in the northern states, but its use was sporadic and confined mostly to rural and poor people. The *chiltepin*, the nation's only wild pepper, does not grow in the North. Puritans discouraged the cultivation of hot peppers, and our founding fathers seem to have eschewed them.

There were, of course, numerous exceptions, many of them were for medical reasons. Brigham Young is said to have used cayenne tea to cure an outbreak of cholera among the Mormon pioneers. Samuel Thomson, a New Hampshire farmer who established a wide practice as an herb doctor in New England, used cayenne extensively in 1810.

But these people, and others like them, were rare. The middle class in North America associated *Capsicum* with poverty and shunned its use as either food or medicine. Piquant foods were relegated to a second-class citizenship in America's kitchens. Garlic and hot peppers became "specialty" items. Their frequent use denoted the sort of backwardness that a deodorized white person expected to find only in minorities like newly arrived immigrants, lower-class black people, or poor white trash. To insist on incorporating hot peppers or garlic into the daily diet was antisocial and verged on being unpatriotic.

This attitude began to change drastically around 1970. So-called "ethnic" cuisines have achieved an unprecedented popularity across the length and breadth of middle-class America. Italian, Chinese, and Mexican food are now a common sight on the dinner table, and there has been a simultaneous proliferation of restaurants offering these dishes. By 1999, the sale of salsas had surpassed those of tomato catsup in the United States. Many of these meals can be prepared almost as cheaply as "fast food," and unlike the greasy cardboard burgers and chemically whitened French fries, they delight the tastebuds with an array of flavors and sensations. Even Cajun food had its day in the sun; in the mid-1980s Cajun cuisine became a national favorite, much to the astonishment of many Acadians. In the long run, it looked like citizens would demand more from their food than something to cram down their gullets as fast as possible.

More and more people in the United States are using some form of hot peppers to flavor their food. While the supply and demand situation has not yet reached a level of scarcity, an annually increasing acreage of *Capsicum* is needed to satisfy the growing national market. From Maine to Oregon, more and more people want hot food, and that is good news to pepper growers.

With the exception of Louisiana, all the states that have traditionally relied on hot peppers as a significant commercial crop are enjoying an annual increase in revenue. The money has never been better. In 1950, California produced $3 million worth of hot peppers. By 1980, that figure had risen to close to $20 million. The varieties being grown are primarily the long green chilies like Anaheims.

Texas is close behind California, and leads the nation in jalapeño production, growing more than all other states combined. New Mexico tripled its pepper acreage between 1950 and 1980. Even Arizona, which always produced limited amounts of *Capsicum*, currently grows more hot peppers than Louisiana. In 1950, when Acadiana's economy depended on farming, it was the nation's largest pepper producer, but now southern Louisiana's prosperity, or lack of it, hinges on what is happening in Tehran on the petroleum market, or on the dollar market in London, and the heyday of its pepper growers has passed.

The expanding United States market for *Capsicum* is still in its nascent phase. To cautiously use a few drops of hot sauce or a dash of cayenne pepper is a far cry from popping a few whole peppers with a late afternoon beer. North Americans need to be encouraged and supported in their burgeoning relationship with the fiery fruits. It is a habit well worth acquiring. It stimulates digestion, clears the sinuses, and seems to be of benefit to the respiratory system.

Equally important, *Capsicum* is a psychotropic plant. It heightens the awareness of a given moment by disrupting normal thought patterns and attention spans. Mundane, temporal consciousness is superseded by a sharp, intense rush of sensation, and attention is focused on the mouth, on the heat and food. It is hard to read the newspaper or dwell on one's usual cares while eating hot peppers. Reality is altered for a moment, and so the peppers fulfill the traditional function of any of the substances with which people have chosen to alter their states of consciousness over the centuries.

Capsicum's psychotropic effects are briefer and less disruptive than those of many other such substances. Hot peppers are also among the safest of these plants. Most of the others — peyote, psilocybin, jimson weed, nightshade, cannabis, coca, poppies, nutmeg, morning-glory seeds, and a whole host of others — have some deleterious effects on the body, if they are used too frequently. Excessive oral use of *Capsicum* has not been proven to be harmful.

In an essay on hot peppers, Dr. Andrew Weil wrote: "He [the chili pepper lover] knows that pain may be transformed into a friendly sensation whose strength can go into making him high. The secret of the trick lies in perceiving that the sensation follows the form of a wave: it builds to a terrifying peak, then subsides, leaving the body completely unharmed. . . . Familiarity with the sensation makes it possible to eat chili at a rate that keeps the intensity constant. One is then able to glide along on the strong stimulation, experiencing it as somewhere between pleasure and pain that enforces concentration and brings about a high state of consciousness. . . .

"Just as I was helped in learning to be a chili lover by spending time around masters of the art, I am now able to help others. I have guided several persons from the initial stages of mouth burning to intermediate and advanced levels of chili eating and am always gratified to watch them discover the joys of this practice and marvel at their new-found abilities. It is always uplifting to conquer something that once seemed unattainable. And it is especially meaningful to see that by a change of mental attitude, perseverance, and openness to new experience one can transform the external world, even to the extent that something previously appearing painful and injurious can become pleasurable and beneficial."

*

As I left New Iberia, I headed east on Main Street, going out of town along the Old Spanish Trail, the same way I had arrived. Past the antebellum mansions with the Bayou Teche running through their back yards, past the last shopping center, housing development, motel, and trailer court to where the cane fields began. I passed an open field where a large black cow stood placidly grazing while a snow-white cattle egret perched on her back. I slowed down for a brief glimpse of the egret's head bobbing in search of ticks. The bird was a graceful, curving white form rising from the massive block of black.

A horn honked and my attention returned to the highway. A pickup pulled out behind me and passed, going about seventy-five. The young driver looked at me balefully as he shot by, wondering why I was poking along. There was a bumper sticker on the back of his truck: Oil Feeds My Family.

Just outside of Franklin, I picked up a middle-aged hitchhiker carrying a small cardboard suitcase. He was from Beaumont, Texas, and was on his way to Morgan City to catch a boat that would take him to an oil rig for a seven-and-seven shift. He told me if I ever wanted a job I should just give him a call and he'd put me in touch with his boss. He insisted on writing his name and phone number down for me. He got out at one of the shipyards on the western edge of Morgan City, where he was to rendezvous with the boat. His last words to me were by way of a warning to watch out for myself around the French Quarter in New Orleans.

That very night I was mugged in the Quarter, on Royal Street. A hand tapped me on the shoulder while I was standing at a corner waiting for the light to change. When I turned around, a man sprayed something in my eyes. It was one of those repellents that are supposed to ward off just such an attack. Capsaicin was probably its active ingredient. While I was temporarily blinded, tears streaming down my face, my assailant went through my pants' pockets, searching for a wallet. I do not carry one, and my cash was in my shirt pocket. He became unnerved when his probing, poking fingers found no trace of money below my waist and I began to yell for assistance. He fled.

I groped my way down the block to Bourbon Street. My eyes burned unbearably, and I wandered, sobbing, through the mob of tourists who nightly thronged the infamous narrow street. This was where they had all been when I was a block away and needed them. The people and lights were blurred and unreal as I lurched, panicked and blind, among them. I finally found the door to a bar and located the men's room, where I put my face under the faucet. The pain gradually subsided and my sight returned. I gave thanks that instead of being knifed or shot, I had merely been given a dose of my own medicine. Within a few minutes, I was feeling well enough to catch a streetcar out to Tipitina's Club, where I danced all night.

LAGNIAPPE*

ot peppers of the species *Capsicum annuum* will grow as far north as the Canadian border. A little research may be needed to find out which varieties grow best in a given location. These were Emmaline Broussard's instructions for growing hot peppers:

Make a bed, about four feet square and six inches deep out of wood. Fill it with fertile soil, on top of which the seeds should be placed and covered lightly. Cover the bed with glass. Seeds should be planted in the bed only after all danger of frost has passed. When the plants are about six inches high, they are ready to be transplanted to the ground. Put them in rows about eighteen inches apart. Weeds should be hoed down immediately, because the plants will die soon if the weeds grow around them.

Samuel Thomson, a New Hampshire farmer turned herbalist, was one of the first Americans to write extensively about *Capsicum*. He was particularly impressed with the healing power of cayenne. Thomson was also one of the first Americans to mention hot sauce. Reprinted below is a section of his book, *The New Guide to Health*, published in 1832:

---

*Pronounced *lahn-yap*, this Louisiana-French word means a little something thrown in at the end for free.

I never had any knowledge of cayenne being useful as a medicine, or that it had ever been used as such, till I discovered it by accident, as has been the case with most other articles used by me. After I had fixed upon a system for my practice of eating peppers, I found much difficulty in getting something that would not only produce a strong heat in the body, but would retain it till the canker could be removed, and the digestive powers restored, so that the food by being properly digested, would retain the natural heat. I tried a great number of articles that were of a hot nature; but could find nothing that would hold the heat any length of time. I made use of mustard, ginger, horse-radish, peppermint, butternut bark, and many other hot things but they were all more or less volatile and would not have the desired effect.

In the fall of the year 1805 I was out in search of Umbil on a mountain in Walpole, New Hampshire. I went into a house at the foot of a mountain to inquire for some rattlesnake oil; while in the house I saw a large string of red peppers hanging in the room which put me in mind of what I had been a long time in search of to retain the internal heat . . . it answered the purpose better than anything else I had made use of. I put it in spirit with the Emetic herb and gave the tincture mixed in a tea of Witch-hazle leaves, and found that it would retain the heat in the stomach after puking; and preserve the strength of the patient in proportion. I made use of it in different ways, for two years, and always with good success.

In the fall of 1807 I was in Newburyport and saw a bottle of cayenne pepper sauce, being the first I had ever seen. . . . From my experiments I became convinced that this kind of pepper was much stronger and would be better for medical use than the common red pepper grown in gardens. Soon after this I was again in Newburyport and made inquiry and found some cayenne; but it was prepared with salt for table use which injured it for medical purposes. I tried it by tasting and selected that which had the least salt in it. I afterwards made use of this article and found it to answer to all the purposes wished and was the very thing I had long been in search of. The next year I went to Portsmouth and made inquiries concerning cayenne and from those who dealt in the article I learned it was brought to this country from Demarara and Jamaica. . . . I became acquainted with a French gentleman who had a brother in Demarara and made arrangements for him to send to his brother and request him to procure some and have it prepared without salt. He did so and sent a box containing about eighty pounds in a pure state.

When I first began to use this article, it caused much talk among the people of Portsmouth and the adjoining towns. The doctors tried to frighten them by telling them that I made use of cayenne pepper as a medicine, and that it would burn up the stomach and lungs as bad as vitriol. The people generally, however, became convinced by using it, that all the doctors said was false, and it only proved their ignorance of its medical virtues and their malignity towards me. It soon came into general use, and the knowledge of its being useful in curing disease was spread all through the country. . . . I have made use of Cayenne in all kinds of disease, and have given it to patients of all ages and under every circumstance that has come under my practice; and can assure the public that it is perfectly harmless, having never known it to produce any bad effects whatsoever. It is no doubt the most powerful stimulant known; its power is entirely congenial to nature, being powerful only in raising and maintaining heat, on which life depends. It is extremely pungent and when taken, sets the mouth, as it were, on fire; this lasts, however, but a few minutes, and I consider it essentially a benefit for its effect on the glands causes the saliva to flow freely and leaves the mouth clean and moist.

The following two recipes are from Emmaline Broussard. She used cayenne peppers, but other hot peppers may be substituted.

PICKLED PEPPERS

Wash green cayenne peppers with cold water, also small green tomatoes and small cucumbers. Let them dry perfectly good. Cut tomatoes in half. Cucumbers, if really tiny, may be used whole. Otherwise cut into pickle size. Cut cayenne in two, removing all seeds from inside. Put a tablespoon of salt at the bottom of a clean, dry jar and fill about three-quarters full with the peppers, cucumbers, and tomatoes. Then fill the jar to the top with white vinegar. Close jar and your pickles are made.

CHOW-CHOW

Wash cayenne peppers and let them drip dry. Use both red and green peppers to produce a nice shade of color. For each quart use about two large white onions. Remove all the seeds from the peppers. Use a meat grinder to grind the onions and peppers together well. Put a tablespoon of salt at the bottom of a clean, dry fruit jar and fill it three-quarters full with the onion and pepper mixture. Fill to the top with white vinegar. Cover. As you use the chow-chow, keep on adding vinegar to the jar.

This recipe is from Katye Joseph of Nashville, a friend of the author.

PEPPER JELLY
3/4 cup sweet peppers
1/4 cup hot peppers
6 1/2 cups sugar
1 1/2 cups vinegar
1 bottle Certo

Grind the peppers together. In a separate container mix the sugar and vinegar. Combine the two mixtures in a pot and bring to a rolling boil. Remove immediately from the heat and let set for five minutes. Remove any scum, add the Certo, put in sterile jars, and seal.

For Christmas, make a batch of this recipe using green sweet peppers and green hot peppers, and add a bit of green food coloring. Make another batch with sweet red peppers and hot red peppers, and add red coloring. Then give a pair of jars as a pretty and practical present. This goes well with any meat, but especially lamb.

BOUDIN BLANC
Makes 3 long sausages
3 foot-long sausage casings
3 pounds lean pork, cut into 1-inch cubes

water
2 large onions, coarsely chopped
6 whole peppercorns
5 teaspoons salt
1 medium bell pepper, coarsely chopped
3 scallions, coarsely chopped
3 garlic cloves, minced
2 1/2 cups cooked white rice
1 teaspoon ground sage
2 1/2 teaspoons cayenne pepper
1/2 teaspoon black pepper

Soak the sausage casings in water for several hours until they are soft. Place the pork in a small Dutch oven and add enough water to cover. Bring the liquid to a boil over high heat and skim the foam. Add one onion, the peppercorns, and 1 teaspoon of salt. Reduce the heat to low, partially cover the pot, and simmer for 90 minutes.

Remove the pork from the liquid and place it in a bowl with the other onion, green pepper, scallions, and garlic. Run this mixture through a food grinder. Then add the rice, sage, cayenne, black pepper, and remaining salt. Beat well until the mixture is thoroughly combined and smooth.

Mount the casings one at a time on the sausage attachment of the meat grinder and spoon the mixture into the mouth of the grinder. Be careful not to fill the casings too tightly or they may burst.

Cook the sausages immediately or refrigerate for several days.

CHICKEN GUMBO

Serves 4

1/2 pound chorizo or other spicy sausage, cut into thin slices
1 cup plus 6 tablespoons white flour
1 teaspoon salt
1 teaspoon freshly ground black pepper
1 3-pound chicken, cut into serving pieces
cooking oil
1 medium onion, finely chopped
2 large celery stalks, finely chopped

1 medium green pepper, finely chopped

2 quarts water

1/4 teaspoon Tabasco Sauce

1/2 teaspoon cayenne pepper

1 1/2 teaspoons filé powder

2 cups cooked white rice

Place the chorizo in a medium frying pan and brown on all sides over medium-high heat. Remove the sausage from the pan and set aside. Mix 1 cup of the flour with the salt and pepper, and roll the chicken pieces in the mixture until thoroughly coated. Then place the chicken in the frying pan, adding oil if necessary, and cook over medium-high heat for 10 minutes or until each piece is browned on all sides.

Make the brown roux by stirring 6 tablespoons of white flour into 6 tablespoons of cooking oil and cooking over low heat, stirring constantly, for about 45 minutes or until the mixture is a rich brown. Use 1/2 cup of the mixture for this recipe and discard the remaining roux.

Pour the roux into a small Dutch oven and warm over medium heat. Add the onion, celery, and green pepper, and sauté over medium-low heat for several minutes or until the onion is golden. Then pour in the water, add the Tabasco Sauce and cayenne, and stir well. Stir in the sausage, add the chicken, and reduce the heat to low. Cover the pot and cook over low heat for 2 hours, stirring occasionally.

Remove the pot from the heat and carefully stir in the filé powder. Do not reheat or the filé will become stringy and unpleasant.

Serve the gumbo at once over mounds of rice spooned into individual serving bowls.

CRAWFISH ÉTOUFFÉE

Serves 4

4 tablespoons flour

4 tablespoons cooking oil

2 stalks celery, finely chopped

1 medium onion, finely chopped

3 scallions, finely chopped

1 1-pound can tomatoes with their juice, finely chopped

1 1/2 cups water

1/2 teaspoon cayenne pepper

1/2 teaspoon Tabasco Sauce

1 1/2 teaspoons salt

1/2 teaspoon freshly ground black pepper

2 cups cooked crawfish meat

2 cups cooked white rice

Over low heat, stir the flour into the oil and cook, stirring constantly, for about 45 minutes or until the roux is a rich brown color. Pour the roux into a small Dutch oven and warm over medium heat. Add the celery, onions, and scallions and stir well. Cook over medium heat, stirring constantly, for several minutes or until the onions are golden. Add the tomatoes and their juice and stir well. Pour in the water and stir in the cayenne, Tabasco, salt, and pepper. Simmer over medium-low heat for 10 minutes, stirring occasionally. Add the crawfish, stir, and cook for five more minutes.

Spoon the rice into each serving bowl, pour the étouffée over it, and serve at once.

RED BEANS AND RICE

Serves 6

2 tablespoons cooking oil

2 tablespoons flour

1 medium onion, finely chopped

1 clove of garlic, minced

large ham bone with scraps of meat still attached

3 cups dried red beans

water

3 cups cooked white rice

Pour the oil into a large Dutch oven and stir in the flour. Combine and cook for two minutes over medium heat. Add the onion and garlic and sauté for several minutes or until the onion is golden.

Place the ham bone in the pan and pour in the beans. Add enough water to cover the beans, and cook over medium-low heat, stirring frequently, for 60 to 90 minutes or until the beans are soft.

Serve the beans over individual portions of rice.

SHELLFISH BOIL

Makes 2 cups

1/2 cup mustard seeds

1/2 cup coriander seeds

3 tablespoons dill seeds

4 tablespoons whole allspice

1 tablespoon whole cloves

6 dried hot chili peppers, coarsely crumbled

2 large bay leaves, coarsely crumbled

Mix all ingredients together until thoroughly blended. Use to season poaching liquid for crawfish, shrimp, or crab.

SHRIMP JAMBALAYA

Serves 4

4 cups water

1/2 teaspoon salt

1 pound medium shrimp, shelled and cleaned

3 tablespoons butter

1 medium onion, finely chopped

2 cloves of garlic, mashed

3 large tomatoes, finely chopped

2 celery stalks, finely chopped

1 medium green pepper, finely chopped

1/2 cup water

1/2 teaspoon cayenne pepper

1 teaspoon salt

1/2 pound ham, diced into 1/2-inch cubes

2 cups cooked white rice

Bring the 4 cups of water to a boil over high heat in a large saucepan and add the salt. Reduce the heat to medium high, add the shrimp, and cook for five minutes or until the shrimp are firm and pink. Remove the shrimp from the poaching liquid and set aside.

Melt the butter in a large frying pan over medium heat and add the onion, garlic, tomatoes, celery, and pepper. Stir well and sauté for several minutes or until the onion is golden. Pour in the 1/2 cup water, stir in the cayenne and salt, and simmer for 5 minutes over medium-low heat. Then stir in the ham and simmer for an additional 5 minutes.

Add the rice and shrimp and stir until thoroughly combined. Put a lid on the pan or transfer to a large Dutch oven and bake at 350 degrees for 20 minutes. Serve at once.

The following recipes come from Joe Cahn at the New Orleans School of Cooking. Joe says, "When you make jambalaya, invite the neighborhood."

GUMBO

Serves 15–20

1 cup oil

1 cup flour

4 cups chopped onion

2 cups chopped celery

2 cups chopped green pepper

1 tablespoon chopped garlic

8 cups seafood stock

6 small crabs, cleaned

1 bay leaf

1/2 teaspoon thyme

salt and pepper, to taste

2 cups chopped green onions

3 pounds peeled shrimp

4 cups sautéed okra

5 to 7 cups cooked rice (optional)

sherry (optional)

filé powder (optional)

In a large soup pot over medium heat, combine the oil and flour to make a roux. Cook at medium heat for 25–35 minutes, stirring constantly, until it is dark brown. Add onions, celery, and green pepper to the roux, and cook briefly. Add the garlic and cook, stirring continuously, until vegetables reach desired tenderness. Gradually stir in liquid and bring to a boil. Add crabs and cook for 1 hour. Add half the bay leaf, the thyme, and salt and pepper (either black or cayenne) to taste. Reduce heat and simmer for an hour or more.

About 10 minutes before serving, add green onions, shrimp, sautéed okra, and remainder of spice. Gumbo may or may not be served over rice. Adding sherry at the table is another option. Have filé powder available for individuals who wish to add it to their gumbo—1/4 to 1/2 teaspoon per serving is recommended.

OKRA SHRIMP GUMBO

Serves 6–8

10 cups okra, sliced into wheels

1 cup oil

4 cups chopped onion

2 cups chopped celery

2 cups chopped green pepper

1 tablespoon chopped garlic

8 cups shrimp stock (or clam juice or use fish bouillon cubes)

2 28-ounce cans tomatoes

3 bay leaves

salt

black pepper

cayenne pepper

thyme

basil

1 cup chopped green onions

1 cup chopped parsley

3 pounds or more raw shrimp, peeled

7 cups cooked rice

Sauté the okra in oil over medium heat until the sliminess begins to disappear. Add onions, celery, green pepper, and garlic; sauté until the vegetables begin to turn transparent. Add the shrimp stock, tomatoes, and bay leaves, and stir in salt, black and cayenne pepper, thyme, and basil to taste. Simmer slowly for 1 to 2 hours; check seasoning. Add green onions, parsley, and shrimp for the last five minutes of cooking. Serve over rice.

TROUT MEUNIÈRE

Serves 4

1/4 cup pecans

4 trout fillets (8 to 10 ounces each)

Creole seasoning, to taste (recipe follows)

1 cup flour

1 cup milk

1 egg

oil for frying

Roast the pecans on a baking sheet in a 350-degree oven for 20 minutes. Set aside. Sprinkle trout fillets with Creole seasoning. Combine about 1 teaspoon Creole seasoning with the flour. Beat the milk, egg, and about 1 teaspoon Creole seasoning together to make an egg wash. In a large skillet over medium-high heat, heat enough oil to come partway up the side of the fillets. Immediately before frying, dip fish into flour, then into egg wash, then into flour again. Fry fillets on one side until golden brown (about 3 minutes), turn, and continue frying until the other side is golden brown. Remove from pan, drain well, and place on serving plates. Spread fillets with pecan butter and top with New Orleans Meunière sauce. Sprinkle with roasted pecans.

PECAN BUTTER

1 cup pecans

1/2 pound unsalted butter, softened

2 tablespoons Worcestershire sauce

1 tablespoon lemon juice

Roast the pecans on a baking sheet in a 350-degree oven for 20 minutes. Put the pecans in a food processor and pulse until they are chopped relatively fine. Add the remaining ingredients and blend thoroughly.

NEW ORLEANS MEUNIÈRE SAUCE

1/4 pound butter

1 tablespoon flour

1/2 cup seafood stock

1 1/2 tablespoons Worcestershire sauce

1 teaspoon lemon juice

1/2 teaspoon Creole seasoning (recipe follows)

Melt 1 tablespoon of the butter in a saucepan over medium heat. Stir in the flour to make a roux. Continue cooking over medium heat for 10 minutes, stirring constantly, until the roux is a medium brown. Add the rest of the butter and remaining ingredients, mix well, and simmer for 5 minutes.

CREOLE SEASONING

Makes a little over 1 cup

1/6 cup salt

1/8 cup powdered or granulated garlic

1/8 cup powdered or granulated onion

2 tablespoons black pepper

1 tablespoon cayenne pepper

1 tablespoon thyme

2 tablespoons oregano

1/4 cup paprika

Combine all ingredients and mix thoroughly. Store in a glass jar. Keeps well.

CHICKEN LAFÊTE

Follow the recipe for Trout Meunière, substituting boned and skinned chicken breasts for the trout fillets. Roast the pecans, season the chicken and the flour, make the egg wash, and coat the chicken breasts as above. Heat about 1 cup oil in a large skillet and sauté the breasts over moderately high heat for 3 to 4 minutes on each side, or until golden brown. Omit pecan butter. Make the New Orleans Meunière sauce using chicken stock in place of seafood stock. Serve the chicken over rice, topped with the sauce and roasted pecans.

SHRIMP CREOLE

Serves 8

3 pounds peeled shrimp

8 tablespoons butter (1/4 pound)

8 tablespoons flour

2 cups chopped onion

1 cup chopped celery

1 cup chopped green pepper

1 tablespoon chopped garlic

3 cups shrimp stock (or clam juice or use fish bouillon cubes)

1 14- to 16-ounce can tomato sauce

1 tablespoon thyme

1 tablespoon basil

3 bay leaves

1 tablespoon brown sugar

4 thin slices lemon

salt, to taste

cayenne pepper, to taste

1 cup chopped green onions

1 cup chopped parsley

6 cups cooked rice

Sauté the shrimp in butter for 2 to 3 minutes over medium heat; remove from pan. Add the flour to the butter and cook over medium heat for 10–15 minutes, stirring constantly, until lightly browned. Add the onion, celery, green pepper, and garlic, and sauté the vegetables until they begin to turn transparent. Add the stock, tomato sauce, thyme, basil, bay leaves, brown sugar, lemon slices, and salt and cayenne pepper. Simmer for about 15 minutes. Add the green onions, parsley, and shrimp for the last 5 minutes of cooking. Serve over rice.

CHICKEN CREOLE

Follow the directions for shrimp Creole, omitting the basil and substituting 3 pounds of boned chopped chicken for the shrimp and chicken stock for the seafood stock.

BAKED CHICKEN WITH HONEY-ALMOND SAUCE

Serves 4

1 chicken, cut in 8 pieces

salt

black pepper

cayenne pepper

3 chicken bouillon cubes

1 1/2 quarts boiling water

3 1/2 ounces sliced almonds

1/2 cup raw honey

1/2 cup cornstarch

Preheat oven to 350 degrees. Season the chicken with salt, black pepper, and cayenne pepper to taste, and bake for 1 hour.

Dissolve bouillon cubes in boiling water. Add 1 teaspoon each salt, black pepper, and cayenne pepper, stir in the almonds and the honey, and mix thoroughly. Return liquid to a rolling boil, and thicken with cornstarch that has been mixed evenly with cold water.

Spoon some of the sauce over the chicken and pass the rest at the table. The chicken may be served over rice and quartered fresh mushrooms, with green snap beans as a side vegetable. Extra sauce can be used for dipping bread.

CORNISH HENS WITH CAJUN NUT STUFFING
AND ORANGE-PINEAPPLE SAUCE

4 teaspoons salt

1 teaspoon black pepper

1/2 teaspoon white pepper

1 teaspoon garlic salt

1/2 teaspoon granulated onion

1/2 teaspoon paprika

1/2 cup onion, finely chopped

1/2 cup celery, finely chopped

1/2 cup green pepper, finely chopped

1/4 pound butter

1 teaspoon garlic, chopped

1 cup bread crumbs

1 cup ground pecans

4 Rock Cornish game hens

1/4 cup chicken stock

Combine the seasonings and mix well; set aside. Mix together the onions, celery, and green pepper, and sauté in the butter over medium heat until limp and brown. Add the garlic, bread crumbs, ground pecans, and the seasoning mixture to taste, and mix well. Sprinkle the game hens inside and out with the seasoning mixture, and fill loosely with the stuffing. Bake in a 350-degree oven, basting frequently with the chicken stock, for 45–60 minutes or until the juices run clear when a small slit is made in the upper thigh.

Spoon some orange-pineapple sauce over each game hen, and pass the rest at the table.

ORANGE-PINEAPPLE SAUCE
3 chicken bouillon cubes
1 1/2 quarts boiling water
1/4 cup domestic rum
2 tablespoons brandy
2 tablespoons light brown sugar
1 6-ounce can orange slices, diced
1 6-ounce can pineapple slices, diced
1/2 cup cornstarch

Dissolve the bouillon cubes in boiling water; combine with rum, brandy, and sugar. Add the diced orange and pineapple and season with the stuffing seasoning mixture to taste. Mix the cornstarch evenly with cold water. Bring sauce to a boil, add cornstarch, and cook, stirring, until it is thickened to your liking.

NEW ORLEANS STYLE BARBEQUED SHRIMP
Serves 8
1 pound butter
1 teaspoon chopped garlic
3 to 4 pounds shrimp
2 tablespoons Creole seasoning (see recipe above) or to taste
5 ounces beer
1/4 cup Worcestershire sauce
1 teaspoon lemon juice

Melt 3/4 pound butter in a large skillet. Sauté garlic, shrimp, and seasoning for 2 to 3 minutes. Add the beer, Worcestershire sauce, and lemon juice, and cook for 3 to 6 minutes, until the shrimp are cooked and the liquid thickens. Add the remaining butter and shake pan until the butter is melted and the mixture becomes creamy. Serve with plenty of French bread to sop up the sauce.

CHICKEN SAUCE PIQUANTE

Serves 8–10

2 pounds boned chicken meat
Creole seasoning (see recipe above)
1/2 pound lard
flour (about 1 cup)
2 cups chopped onion
2 cups chopped celery
2 cups chopped green pepper
1 tablespoon chopped garlic
1 29-ounce can tomato sauce
1 29-ounce can crushed tomatoes
2 cups chicken stock
2 to 3 tablespoons dark brown sugar, to taste
2 to 3 bay leaves
1 teaspoon thyme
1 teaspoon oregano
2 teaspoons sweet basil
1 to 2 teaspoons salt, to taste
1 to 2 teaspoons cayenne pepper, to taste

Season the chicken well with Creole seasoning or any blend of your choice, and brown it in the lard over medium-high heat. Remove chicken from the pan. Measure the fat, return it to the pan, and make a roux by stirring in an equal amount of flour. Cook over medium heat 12–14 minutes, stirring constantly, until the roux is medium brown. Add onion, celery, and green pepper, and cook briefly, add the garlic and sauté vegetables over medium heat until tender. Stir in the tomato sauce, crushed tomatoes, chicken stock, and enough brown sugar to cut the acid taste of the tomatoes. Return chicken to the pan, add the seasonings, and simmer until the sauce has thickened and the chicken is tender. Serve over rice.

Serves 6–8

24 ounces artichokes canned in water, quartered

1 quart strong chicken stock or chicken stock substitute *

2 cups chopped green onions

salt, to taste

cayenne pepper, to taste

1 teaspoon thyme leaves

1/4 cup melted butter

1/4 cup plus 1 tablespoon flour

1 quart heavy cream

2 dozen (1 quart) oysters (shrimp or scallops may be substituted)

1 tablespoon chopped parsley

Combine the artichokes, stock, 1 cup of the green onions, salt, cayenne pepper, and thyme in a large pot and bring to a boil. Reduce heat and simmer for 12 minutes. In a small saucepan, combine melted butter and flour and cook over medium heat, stirring constantly, for 2 to 3 minutes, to make a light roux. Add the roux to the simmering pot, stir in the heavy cream, and simmer for 10 minutes. Add the oysters and simmer 5 more minutes. Serve garnished with parsley and the remaining green onions.

BASIC CREOLE SAUCE

Makes 2 quarts

1/2 cup oil

1/2 cup flour

1 cup chopped onion

1/2 cup chopped celery

1/2 cup chopped green pepper

2 cloves garlic, chopped

2 14- to 16-ounce cans tomato sauce

1/2 teaspoon thyme

3 bay leaves

*Chicken stock substitute can be made by draining the liquid from the oysters and/or the artichokes.

1/2 teaspoon cayenne pepper

salt, to taste

1 tablespoon brown sugar

1/2 cup chopped shallots or green onions

1/2 cup parsley

Heat the oil in a saucepan. Add the flour to make a roux, and cook over medium heat 12–15 minutes, stirring constantly, until it is medium brown. Add the onions, celery, green pepper, and garlic, and sauté until the vegetables are tender. Blend in the tomato sauce, seasonings, and brown sugar, and simmer for about 15 minutes. Five minutes before serving, add the shallots and parsley. Serve with chicken, plain over rice, or with any meat.

JAMBALAYA

Serves 12

1 chicken, boned and cut up

salt and pepper, to taste

1/4 cup oil, lard, or bacon drippings

1 1/2 pounds sausage

1 heaping tablespoon brown sugar

4 cups chopped onion

2 cups chopped celery

2 cups chopped green pepper

1 tablespoon chopped garlic

5 cups chicken stock

2 heaping teaspoons salt

cayenne pepper, to taste

Kitchen Bouquet (optional)

4 cups long-grain rice

2 cups chopped green onions

3 chopped tomatoes (optional)

Season chicken with salt and pepper and sauté in oil over medium-high heat. Add the sausage and sauté until browned; remove chicken and sausage from pot. For brown jambalaya, add the brown sugar to the hot oil and stir until caramelized. (You may also either substitute

Kitchen Bouquet for the brown sugar or add flour to the oil to make a brown roux.) Add the onion, celery, green pepper, and garlic, and sauté until the onions are translucent.

Return the chicken and sausage to the pot. Add the stock, salt, cayenne pepper, and other seasonings as desired, and bring to a boil. (You will need to overseason in order to compensate for the rice.) If desired, add 1 to 2 tablespoons Kitchen Bouquet. Add rice and return to a boil; cover and reduce heat.

Simmer for a total of 30 minutes. After ten minutes of cooking, remove cover and quickly turn rice from top to bottom completely. Add green onions and (if desired) chopped tomatoes.

For red jambalaya: proceed as for brown jambalaya, above, but omit the brown sugar and the (optional) Kitchen Bouquet, and add 1/4 cup paprika to the stock and other seasonings before adding the rice. You may also want to use half stock and half tomato juice or V-8 for your cooking liquid.

BIBLIOGRAPHY

Acosta, Joseph de. *The Natural and Moral History of the Indies.* New York: Burt Franklin Publishing Co., 1970.

Bernard, Rosemary Eckart. "A Biography of the Youth of Edward Avery McIlhenny." Master's thesis, University of Southwestern Louisiana, 1969.

Berry, Wendell. *The Unsettling of America: Culture and Agriculture.* San Francisco: Sierra Books, 1977.

Blom, Frans F. *The Conquest of Yucatan.* New York: Houghton Mifflin Publishing Co., 1936.

Blot, W. J., et al. "Geographic Patterns of Lung Cancer: Industrial Correlations." *American Journal of Epdemiology* 103 (June 1976): 539–50.

Byers, Douglas S., ed. *The Prehistory of the Tehuacan Valley.* Austin: University of Texas Press, 1967.

Candolle, Alphonse Louis Pierre Pyramus de. *Origin of Cultivated Plants.* New York: Hafner Publishing Co., 1959.

Chatterton, Harry J. "Pepper Production in Southern Louisiana." *Journal of Geography,* December 1939, 364–69.

Clevinger, Thomas S. "A History of Vegetable Crops in New Mexico." *New Mexico Agricultural Experiment Station Bulletin No. 624.* Las Cruces: April 1974.

Cockerill, P. W. "Economics of the Production and Marketing of Chile in New Mexico." *New Mexico State University Agricultural Experiment Station Bulletin No. 314.* Las Cruces: April 1944.

Columbus, Christopher. *Personal Narrative of the First Voyage of Columbus to America.* Boston: Thomas B. Wait and Son, 1827.

Cruz, Martin de la. *The Badianus Manuscript.* Baltimore: Johns Hopkins University Press, 1940.

Davenport, William Albert. "The Domestication of the *Capsicum* Peppers." Master's thesis, University of Oregon, 1971.

Felger, Richard, and Robert Curtis Wilkinson. "Feast of Life." *CoEvolution Quarterly,* Fall 1978.

Fowler, Cary. *Reaping What We Sow.* The Frank Porter Graham Center in Wadesboro, North Carolina, 1979.

Grieve, Maud. *A Modern Herbal.* New York: Dover Books, 1971.

Hallowell, Christopher. *People of the Bayous.* New York: Dutton Publishing Co., 1979.

Hamill, K. "Enchantment in the Louisiana Marshes." *Fortune,* October 1965, 158–64.

Heiser, Charles B., Jr. *Nightshades—The Paradoxical Plant.* San Francisco: W. H. Freeman and Co., 1969.

Heiser, Charles B., Jr., and Barbara Pickersgill. "Names for the Bird Peppers." *Baileya* 19 (1975): 151–56.

Heiser, Charles B., Jr., and Paul G. Smith. "The Cultivated *Capsicum* Peppers." *Economic Botany* (1953): 214–26.

Kane, Harnett T. *The Bayous of Louisiana.* New York: William Morrow and Co., 1943.

Ketusinh, Ouay, et al. "Influence of *Capsicum* Solution on Gastric Oddities." *American Journal of Proctology* 17, no. 6 (1966): 511–16.

Kneeder, H. S. *Through Storyland to Sunset Seas.* Cincinnati: A. H. Pugh Printing Co., 1899.

Latorre, Dolores and Felipe. "Plants Used by the Mexican Kickapoo Indians." *Economic Botany* (1977): 348.

MacFadyen, J. Tevere. "A Battle Over Seeds." *The Atlantic Monthly,* November 1985.

McNulty, J. "Our Footloose Correspondent." *The New Yorker,* June 13, 1953.

McPhee, John. *Oranges.* New York: Farrar, Straus and Giroux, 1967.

Nabhan, Gary. "Chiltepines!" *El Palacio* 84, no. 2 (1978).

Narayananda, Swami. *Bramacharya—Its Necessity and Practice for Boys and Girls.* Rishikesh, India: N. K. Prasad and Co., 1960.

Ovideo, Gonzalo Fernández de. *Natural History of the West Indies.* Translated and edited by Sterling Stoudemire. Chapel Hill: University of North Carolina Press, 1959.

Parkinton, John. *Theatricum Botanicum.* London: Thomas Cotes, 1640.

Pickersgill, Barbara. "The Domestication of Chili Peppers." In *The Domestication and Exploitation of Plants and Animals,* edited by Peter J. Ucko and A. W. Dimbleby, 443–50. Chicago: Aldine Publishing Co., 1969.

Puckett, Newbell Niles. *Folk Beliefs of the Southern Negro.* Chapel Hill: University of North Carolina Press, 1926.

Reilly, Timothy, F. "Early Acadiana Through Anglo-Saxon Eyes, Part II." *Atakapas Gazette,* Fall 1977.

Ries, Maurice. *The 100 Year History of Tabasco.* Avery Island: The McIlhenny Company, 1968.

Riks, Dolf. "About Sambal and Nam Prik." *Bangkok Post,* December 21, 1975.

Roys, Ralph L. *The Ethnobotany of the Maya.* New Orleans: Tulane University Press, 1931.

Rushton, William F. *Cajuns: From Acadiana to Louisiana.* New York: Farrar, Straus and Giroux, 1979.

Russell, Lisa C., and Kim J. Burchiel. "Neurophysiological Effects of Capsaicin." *Brain Research* 320, no. 2-3 (1984): 165–76.

Scully, Virginia. *Treasury of American Herbs.* New York: Crown Publishing Co.,
    1970.

Sterba, James P. "An Authority on Chilies." *New York Times*, Sept. 14, 1975, 46.

Sturtevant, Edward Lewis. *Sturtevant's Edible Plants of the World.* Edited by U. P.
    Hedrick. New York: Dover Publications, 1972.

Sutton, H. "Sweet and Hot." *Saturday Review*, January 15, 1966, 46–47.

Texas Pepper Foundation (Weslaco, Texas). *News Letter*, Fall, 1977.

Tolbert, Frank X. *A Bowl of Red.* New York: Doubleday Publishing Co., 1972.

Towle, Margaret. *The Ethnobotany of Pre-Columbian Peru.* New York:
    Wenner-Gren Foundation of Anthropological Research, 1961.

Trillin, Calvin. "U.S. Journal: Morgan City, La." *The New Yorker*, January 15,
    1979, 90–93.

Tyler, M. L. *Homeopathic Drug Pictures.* Rustington, Sussex, England: Health
    Sciences Press, 1942.

Viranuvatti, Vikit, et al. "Effects of Capsicum Solution on Human Gastric
    Mucosa." *The American Journal of Gastroenterology*, 58:227–32.

Vogel, Virgil J. *American Indian Medicine.* Norman: University of Oklahoma
    Press, 1970.

Weil, Andrew. *The Marriage of the Sun and the Moon.* New York: Houghton Mifflin
    Publishing Co., 1980.

Whiteside, Thomas J. "A Reporter at Large (Tomatoes)," *The New Yorker*,
    January 24, 1977, 36–61.

INDEX

tion of, 4, 139–41; introduction in Europe, 9–10; introduction in Asia, 11; as medicine, 11, 19, 87–88; addiction to, 11, 23; and vitamins A and C, 11–12, 139; cultivation of in southern Louisiana, 23, 24–25, 26, 35, 110, 140–41; pickers/picking of, 23, 106; cultivation of in Iberia Parish, 24; production of in southwestern United States, 30, 35, 37, 110, 139, 140–41; production of in Latin America, 35, 37, 119; and asthma, 78, 88; and coughs and colds, 87, 88; and alcoholic gastritis, 87–88, 94; and aches and pains, 88–89; as a weapon, 89–90; as protection against dogs, 90; as punishment, 90; and menstruation, 98; as aphrodisiacs, 98, 99–100; and sex, 98–99; and male genito-urinary problems, 99; and agribusiness, 110, 123–24; variety Numex Big Jim, 118; and seed selection, 123–24, 125; psychotropic effects of, 141–42. See also *Capsicum*; Cayenne peppers; Jalapeño peppers; Tabasco peppers

Hot sauce, 99, 117, 144; popularity of, 23, 36; marketing of, 36, 92–93; manufacture of, 36–38. *See also* Tabasco Sauce

Huaca Prieta, Peru: archaeological site at, 18

Indonesia, 138–39

Jalapeño peppers, 23–24, 34, 110, 141; use of in making hot sauce, 36, 37, 117

Jambalaya (recipe), 161–62; shrimp (recipe), 151–52

Jefferson Island, 62, 63, 64, 115

Las Casas, Bartolomeo de, 9

Leprosarium, 72–74

Leprosy, 72–74

Long, Huey, 28

Lung cancer: in southern Louisiana, 70–71, 79–80

McIlhenny, Edmund (company founder), 34, 44–45

McIlhenny, Edmund (company vice-president in 1980s), 47, 48, 49, 50–51, 55–56

McIlhenny, Edward Avery (Ned), 45–47

McIlhenny, John, 45

McIlhenny, Paul, 47, 48, 50–51

McIlhenny, Walter S., 43–44, 47, 48, 64, 67, 91, 94–95, 111–12, 114–15

McIlhenny Company: product(s) of, 17, 34, 48, 93; as grower and processor of tabascos, 38–39, 41–42, 44–45, 49–57, 62–70, 118, 119; in Latin America, 40, 54, 57, 64–69, 118; history of, 44–48; and nuclear waste, 114

Mayas: use of *Capsicum* by, 18–20, 123

Mechanical harvesting, 23–24, 40–41, 62–64, 110

Meunière sauce, New Orleans (recipe), 154–55

Minanghabau: use of *Capsicum* by, 138

Mexico: use of hot peppers in, 3, 4, 12, 18–20, 94; production of hot peppers in, 35, 37, 39, 65, 66–67

Morgan City, La.: location of, 6; petroleum industry in, 6–7, 28,

38–39, 41–42, 44–45; picking of, 24–25, 39–40, 49–54, 60–62, 87; and Trappey and Sons, 25, 38; cultivation of on Avery Island, 38, 39, 49–50, 54, 66, 110, 118; production of in Latin America, 39, 54, 57, 64–69, 118; derivation of name of, 45; and sinus conditions, 57; cultivation of on Jefferson Island, 62, 63, 64; viruses and insects affecting, 65–66, 118–19; seed for growers of, 118; Greenleaf, 119

Tabasco Sauce, 15, 17; history of, 34, 44–45; popularity of, 42, 93; history of name of, 45; manufacture and aging of, 56–57, 91; production figures for, 68–69; sales of, 69, 93; marketing of, 93; color of, 117; freezing point of, 117; percentage of capsaicin in, 117

Tehuacan, Mexico: archaeological site at, 18

Thailand, 93, 139

Thomson, Samuel, 140, 144–46

Tipitina's Club, 137, 143

Tobacco, 11, 66

Tomatoes, 41

Trappey, B. F., 34

Trappey, W. J., 35–36, 111

Trappey and Sons, Inc., 34–37, 78, 93, 117–18

Trout Meunière (recipe), 154

Valium, 107

Venezuela, 39, 65, 68

Vermilion Bay, 30

Vitamin A, 11–12, 139

Vitamin C, 11–12, 139

Weeks Island, 113, 115, 135

Witches, 82

Women: as pepper pickers, 50; in southern Louisiana, 95, 107–8; in sugar cane mills, 106–7

Young, Brigham, 140

Ziment, Irwin, 19–20, 88

Zimbabwe, 93–94